For Veloria

"Breast cancer thought it took my aunt

She merely went home."

-"If Tomorrow isn't Promised"

To ANDREW
THANKS FoR the ~~support~~
Much Love
Samuel K Hawkins

Original and modified cover art by Samuel Hawkins, Victoria Caldwell
and CoverDesignStudio.com
Editing by Donna Hawkins and Levi McDuffee

Printed in the United States of America

First Printing, 2013

ISBN 978-0615871318

River City Poetry
Paducah, KY 42001

Ordering Information:
Quantity sales. Special discounts are available on quantity purchases by
corporations, associations, and others. For details, contact the publisher by
email.
Orders by U.S. trade bookstores and wholesalers. Please contact Big
Distribution: via email

www.samuelhawkins.com.

www.rivercitypoetry.com

poetry@samuelhawkins.com

samuelhawkins@live.com

THIS IS WHY KIDS WANNA STAY UP LATE

Contribute To Creation

∞

Samuel Hawkins II

Contents

Didn't Do It by Myself

These poems are dedicated to the many cries to God lingering on thirsty lips, born within languages my ears would not readily recognize. This is for my father and his eternal support. If I had one wish, it would be for a son to see me with at least half of the respect, love, pride, and adoration I have for my father. Thank you Daddy. Without you I wouldn't be here.

A series of these poems are directly derived from the Murray State Women's Center's unfailing drive to raise awareness of domestic violence, sexual assault, child abuse, and violence against humanity. Thank you for your invitations to speak and share my words at Take Back the Night. Jane Etheridge, you are one of the most wonderful and empathetic individuals that I've met to date. Thank you for your service to this world.

This book would not be possible without God's unfailing love, and my family's humbling salt water nose refreshing truth. Samantha, thanks for being my big little sis and composing an impeccable and illustrious illustration of what it means to live up to your fullest potential. When I was younger, I made it a hobby to, "get on yo nerves," and for those who severely lack slang rhetoric we'll say I was driving you insane. Thank you for all of the love and support I don't deserve. Bro, or should I say K-Hawk? Thanks for always challenging me to be better than my best and do more than my mind could conceive. Because of your unsettling question, "So, are you going to keep all of those poems in your head or let the world hear them?" I didn't settle. If it wasn't for you, I'd be satisfied caught within complacency's cage of dead dreams and regret's offspring. After you read this book, I hope you make the choice to sing more, because you possess a golden voice that I know the world would enjoy; and I almost forgot but I'm going to need a book to drip from your pen tip, as well.

Once again I must thank my father (it never ends). Pops, thanks for introducing me to jazz so with my own ears I could see sound transformed into trinkets of auditory bliss. Without my adolescent introduction to jazz, my journey as an artist may have been nonexistent. These words are definitely dedicated to any artist of any age practicing their craft and expressing themselves within any medium. This book was created to arouse the notion that those before our births, all 6.7 billion of us, and the endless numbers to come have an innate inclination to contribute to creation in a special way. I truly believe everyone has a unique voice to add to the chaos, and despite the doubts manifested by way of external or internal negative reinforcement, it is not a must that you inhale dream killing mantra. What you have to say, paint, or capture within a lens could affect a life.

One of the most beautiful sights you can see on this planet is someone embracing their God given talents to leave a mark of magnificent glory for this world to see. So, to any artist who has genuinely created to give this world something beautiful, I thank you.

Without God, this book and every endeavor I've ever conceptualized would be moot. God, thank you for your grace, mercy, and gifts you've bestowed upon me. Please keep me grounded humbly seeking where Your will wants me. In the midst of the popular misconception conceived by the words you've given me, you know and I know that I am far from perfection's rosy aroma discarded within its golden commode. I am a bag of bones seeking Your light as righteous as the rest of us trying to find You within a reflection we willfully distort at times. The moment we lose control and let You shine we'll find Your face and the peace promised.

Dear Mama,

Thank you for always supporting and encouraging me to pursue poetry even when I didn't believe in myself. Thanks for the road trips and the honest heart to hearts that inspired the honesty within the words this world will see or hear. I am blessed that you and my father decided to take Sam, Ken, and me on trips to see this beautiful world. It opened my mind, body, and soul to different cultures, perspectives, and people beyond my hometown.

You act a fool sometimes but I know you are 100% yourself and I respect and love this characteristic about you. Even though you and my father didn't stay together, you both manage to inject love into my life. I just pray I've reciprocated the love received. Without you I don't exist. Thanks for abstaining from alcohol and cigarettes while my brother and I resided within your womb. I need every neuron to remember some of the more lengthy poems within my collection.

Contribute to Creation

Your Son

(insert pet name)

Paducah has poetry!

I started writing poetry in 2001 but I wasn't introduced to my hometown's scene until May 2008. **Niaz, Happy Niaz Kadem Day, and thank you** for the invitation to Etcetera's Friday night open mic. That first summer of 4 open mics a week and even 5 some weeks was critical within my development as an artist. By no means have I scrapped the heels of the pinnacle of poetry but without that summer I wouldn't be who I am. **Sarah, Stacie, E-Red, Alica, Jay, JP, Gabe, Niaz, Capone, Bre, Kristen, and anyone else who has exposed their soul behind the microphone. Thank you for sharing and listening.**

How did I start writing poetry? The truth is always funnier than a lie. This thanks goes out to a special lady who cracked my heart like a California fault line. Without this ridiculous high school crush I possessed and propelled toward an abominable locomotive of rejection this book's birth would've been aborted before conception. But on the contrary, all of high school wasn't infinitely sown within sorrow. Someone brought to my attention a school club in which students came together to share poems they had written. Thus, I became the only football player in the poetry club; dichotomy incarnate. Out of this magnificent club I must give special thanks to Jesse Calhoun (Calholigan!). ACT-SO was fun in so many facets I'd need Goro and Sheva to help me count if my arithmetic abilities are limited to my phalanges. I will not mention every detail in an attempt to keep the paragraph PG, however the experience fertilized my drive to write and I thank you for being my poetry partner. Vanessa Blades, thank you for handing me the book "Said the Shotgun to the Head," by Saul Williams. The words literally changed my life. Greer, all I can give is infinite gratitude for your immortal support and encouragement. Your words were and forever will be glucose to my tulips.

E-Man! Otherwise known as Emmanuel Tavares, your name means God and I do without the slightest seedling of doubt within my garden of thoughts believe you were sent to encourage, inspire, and guide me. The words you gave me were more valuable than platinum or a barrel of black gold. You always convinced me that I could do and be better than what I expected from myself. Without your mountain-size serving of support poetry would only be a dammed river decaying within the lines of my palm. You may refuse to believe it but you are a gifted writer and I pray that you continue to write and inspire despite the humble hymns you hum riddled with lyrics that don't give you the credit you deserve.

Pilot, "NO" was never an option for this book. Thank you for painting the picture of consistent persistence with your much needed advice. You've always inspired me to walk with confidence unafraid to speak my voice clearly and decisively. Your suggestions were a catalyst for my audacity's birth within my words. It's time for another road trip.

To every adolescent eye taking the time to read these words, thank you. This book would be impossible without the many youth I've met along the way on this over-hyped road to adulthood. Thank you for reminding me to remember how to dream and see with a fresh perspective as the years pass.

All things are possible with Christ at the center. God, thank you for writing empathetic sentiments on the sands of my heart, even though I thought my kindness was a weakness, You had a grander purpose than I could have comprehended. "Before any journey ends it must begin" is what you answered when I was praying for guidance so many years ago. I pray this book gives You glory and if only one soul is touched, I've done more than enough.

"Red-line" aka Aunt Donna. Thank you for your time and changing my "that's" to "who's." I love you and Uncle Henderson and thanks for the love and support you've always given me.

Levi, thanks for reading through the book and contributing to creation all those Friday nights. I can't wait to read 2nd fiddle in one of your books. I love you, man. If you ever need anything you know who to call. That's right, Ghost Busters! No, but really I'm here for you if it's in my power.

THIS IS WHY KIDS WANNA STAY UP LATE

Contribute To Creation

This is Why Kids Wanna Stay up Late

"Illuminated Darkness" pen sketch by Samuel Hawkins

Part 1 Illuminated Darkness

B elow the pits of our pores at our very core contains a desire to create. When I was four I built cities with blocks until I graduated to Lego. Before blocks or Lego I'd scribble unflawed images that may, or may have not resembled my family. Even at this age we can see art is essential because it provides an outlet to fundamentally and freely express how we view the world. Without artistic exercise our perspectives petrify while our casket driven imaginations ignite the lie that...nothing changes. Nothing new, ever.

Your very existence expels this exhortation. There is no one like you and there will never be another. Knowing this, I wanted to create something. Something magnificent, something beautiful, something moving, something accessible, something personal, something honest, something unapologetically pure from the shores of my heart thrusted into a sea of cynics, because some will treat this "Snowflake theory" like a root canal recommendation from the dentist.

If our clothes, cars, IPhones, laptops, dwelling spaces, make-up on our faces, and other frivolous facets intertwined within the "America way" don't define us, what does? This "American way" has nothing to do with being American. A synonym for this phrase is an unconditional consumer. Only the poor and unspoiled youth are forced to face this truth the rest of us choose. What defines us? There is nothing ordinary about you. We all have an innate desire and need to create. Whether we cultivate or crush that potential within ourselves and others is a choice we must all make.

As children our imaginations sang pure like the sunrise of an undiscovered island. Completely and uninhibitedly dreaming themes never seen, and by all means it is very important and necessary to allow ideas and the skill set to express these ideas; to develop, grow, and mature. However, there is a gargantuan gap between renovating ideas versus replacing pure thoughts with the status quo. Dare to be different if that inkling exists. Don't miss the opportunity to leave a genuine imprint of what your heartspeaks.

Awaken and give rise to the light burning between your rib-cages. Found within the chambers of our hearts is a dreamer and a creator. There's an

2

endless supply of possibilities and perspectives to infinitely express. The creative process is an unending one. Think about it. How many sunsets has God painted today? The sun is always setting and rising in different locations and within each location the picture painted differs on a daily basis. Marching to monotony reproducing images of suggested success, we may miss that beauty. Not only do our souls long to appreciate this beauty but they yearn to take part and create. Those of us who indecisively harness this energy churning like kaleidoscope roses become vain critics or hecklers who don't create. Within the factories' of our hearts, bubbling below the darkness of doubt are dancers, pianist, violinist, painters, poets, singers, composers, sculptors, orators, and writers with books that beckon to be heard. Hear the light crawling from a casket of "what could of have beens." Contribute to creation. Let the light inside your heart burn blue with desires God has placed throughout your heart.

Before we were seduced to march with the writhing rhythms of sardonic snares, before we didn't care, before apathetic arrogance aroused our interest we were unconsciously willing to share the inner-images of our heart's canvas. Be unafraid of vain critics who pillage passion. Don't Stop, and never denounce your desire to contribute to creation. Create to give, create to give something back, something beautiful, something magnificent, something moving, something accessible, something personal, something honest, something true, something new, something.

3

The Light

I never thought pleasure

Could genocide dreams.

Then again,

A generation inseminated by fleeting themes

Will generate feins.

Incinerated serenity

Slain on the scene of our heart's hope.

We are

Stubborn Stallions

Unlassoed

By Heaven's rope.

But, we all got a lil light táh shine

So maybe it broke.

Mesmerized by lies in our eyes,

We sanitize sights of light

Whispering, humbling hymns

Through the holes of our souls.

We hostage our hearts, regretting a perpetual past praying for a better start.

But we only have now.

So let's move forward like time only has one gear.

If you need change in your life,

You don't necessarily have to wait until the New Year.

This is Why Kids Wanna Stay up Late

So, Cheers, Cheers toss a toast to the future!

Pop a bottle of youth and kiss glasses!

I read in Cosmo we can all be young and party forever.

Like a deaf frat boy, Don't Stop; Continue to fill glasses

and as this, barrage of bullets zips passed us,

We forget, that we all

Have an unavoidable appointment with an empty casket.

Depressing.

But whether you're terminally ill or born yesterday

There is life to live and tales to tell.

Like that time an Italian beauty suggested I propose when I visited South Beach.

Or like that time

Gravity was gorging on stubborn bricks and a friend decided to reach,

Pulling like "lovesmes" and "lovesmenots"

Plucking you like the petal of a gray daisy

From the snares of sorrow.

Or like that time

The doctors daunting diagnosis

Made you fall in love with the scent of tomorrow.

O how we love, the beauty unpromised.

Or like that time

Cancer never had a chance in the fight,

because a family's support was always there

Contribute to Creation

Like snow on a blue artic night.

Our struggles

Unite our existence.

But like missing children posters

Our stories shrivel like a rose draped in winter.

Untold like truth twisting on a devil's lips.

The lies are clouds, and tears rip cheeks like glaciers

When there aren't any more secrets our eyes can hold.

What are you hiding?

Our lives' vacancies?

Empty

Like Las Vegas church pews.

But it's easy to forget hymns for worship

While Saturday sings proven promises of something to do.

And it's hard to seetruth.

Allergic to light.

Therefore we invite darkness.

Ungrowing empathy like newborn seeds on a water free diet.

Resurrected heartless.

And we all ache to be a part of this,

The party

Living life on the edge forever young never dead.

Know-it-all ears mute messages while fun forgets what God said.

Ignorantly Invincible

What are principles?

Without guidance

Our spirits are decrepit elementary schools

Without principals.

If we are, the sacred temples, versus the barren buildings

We visit, and have gone to

For centuries and centuries.

Our Christ-like tendencies should be woven within

The fabric of our DNA

Like the chicken-pox remedy.

But light serves truth

So we tend to see this bright brilliance as an enemy.

Defending the same energies

That sentenced our purity, to our anxiety's penitentiary.

Damned by God.

And Jesus said don't mention me

If our conversations come as often as the ocean breeze in the state of Tennessee.

When we inhale darkness,

We are flinging our nubs

Trying to fly with clipped wings.

Slitting our throats, bleeding heavenly notes

Contribute to Creation

Wishing we could sing.

We are insomniacs

Stalkers of the night, slayers of the light

Who never dream.

Racing head first to a bottomless Nothingness.

Insatiably searching for sorrow.

Because patience went out of style like childhood and Myspace messages.

I never thought these pleasures

Could genocide our dreams.

The insults soaking within the scent of cynics sent to exalt our image.

The empty liquor bottles

The hollow image of success that we follow.

The cat and mouse chase of the night

And the empty sex that follows.

The church gossip that dissolves slow.

Like crashing moons dancing to destruction

We rewrite instructions and determine our purpose and function.

Why do we have to know everything about everything

Except

What lives at the center of our hearts?

Deceiving discipline

Soliciting sin.

Your heart

Is speaking

Listen in.

A little bit about Myself

I like cannolis

Deep-dish pizza

Philly cheesesteaks,

and let's not forget the chicken and waffles.

What can I say?

I'm a fan of foods found in specific geographic locations

It makes me feel at home, even when I'm not at home.

When I'm at home, during morning meditations like a newborn's lungs embracing oxygen for the first time,

I twist open my blinds and breath in sunlight like it's the Word of God.

It helps me hear my heartspeak whispers of wisdom I didn't know I knew.

In fact, I don't.

Like most Christians, and good people I know,

I need *SA*.

Sinners Anonymous, "My name is Samuel Hawkins, and I'm addicted to hypocrisy."

(Hi Samuel)

Well, lets just say I have trouble reciprocating the words I facilitate,

But it illustrates the struggles we all strive to overcome.

And being young is no excuse if you know truth.

The gentlest summer rain will feel like a hurricane

If you build those four walls of faith within your heart without a roof.

I've been there, whole truth, I still loiter but I'm learning, to listen, the love, of a father is my corner.

So, I know nothing is impossible like Philippians 4:13,

And like John 3:16, my Dad taught me the true meaning of sacrifice.

No wonder my favorite color was red.

Still red.

Red like

Stoplights in the hearts of hope lost on the corner of "Not again" and "Another bad breakup."

I can't stop loving her.

My ex.

It sounds pathetic, but my grandmother said

"It's a blessing to love those who don't love you back."

But I don't think that's what she had in mind.

See, her wisdom is like a Rubik's cube

Except, all of the sides are the same color.

If I simply take a step back and quit trying to figure it out

I would begin to understand.

That's the advice she gave me for when I read the Bible.

That's the advice I give my kids when I teach them poetry.

When I teach them poetry they ask, "Mr. Hawkins, how do you remember all this poem rap stuff in yo head?"

And I tell them, Discipline, Dedication, Devotion, and more practice and more practice and more practice and more

Contribute to Creation

But, within the gospels of instant gratification it says nothing about waiting.

So, of course these adolescent ears don't hear me or believe me and I'm crazy so I say

You got me kids.

I love lying to children.

And if I loved lying to children

I would tell them.

"You are nothing, and there is nothing you can do to make a difference

There is nothing different or unique about you."

Since we know this is untrue, let me share a truth with you.

Every time I step behind a mic

Every time I open my mouth, I never stop getting nervous.

I'm just getting better at lying.

Or maybe I'm getting better at trying.

Let's never get tired of trying.

Let's stop planting our quarters beneath gardens lotto ticket-wishing money would begin to grow on trees.

Because if money grew on trees

What would we actually do?

Except for what we love,

because they say a job isn't a job unless you're miserable.

If that's the case I hope I hate reciting poetry and helping young children for the rest of my life.

And for the rest of my life, for better or worse

This is Why Kids Wanna Stay up Late

I may be single.

If you didn't know, I'm a lot of short and a little awkward.

My first date conversations are always awful, like Christmas carols before autumn.

Critics call me rough around the edges,

but the fans think I'm awesome.

Which matters most?

Neither.

What do I think?

I would tell you

But I'm not good with answers

Much better with questions like a Jeopardy all-star.

For example,

A father figure to most dads like his life is a class teaching men how to raise men.

The Question to this answer is

"Who is my father?"

A question I never had to ask, because he was always there

Like awkward silence within a poem you haven't fully memorized yet.

But life is not about perfection

Perseverance.

So like you're a black grandmother's will in the 1960's

Keep going, never stop,

Contribute to Creation

And you don't have to guess.

100 percent correct.

When the answer comes from Alex Trebek, and he says, "Yes."

Buzz in, and answer.

Am I good enough?

Am I beautiful?

Can I catch the stars and give wishes to starving children?

You were never unequipped.

Our frailty frames the picture depicting our power.

Because we can die

We must fight to live.

This is for the life in your veins.

This is for the pains that gave you power.

This was just a little bit about myself

I hope that you can relate.

This poem was conceived from a conversation between the creator and the created. Have you ever heard God's voice? What did it sound like? If God could only text we'd talk more. Abuse of our modern-day innovations brews the recipe for a culture of convenience. What's wrong with that? Like lovers lost, we yearn for more, but video games, Viagra commercials, and reality shows offer immediate comfort, dead soon resurrected as questions. Questions like, what will make me happy? Simple, but like a blind philosophy student handed a basketball given by God, the answers feel undecipherable. Shoot with faith, you can't miss if the rim is the Grand Canyon, but you won't know until you let go.

This is Why Kids Wanna Stay up Late

I didn't sleep last night.

No really, I didn't.

One would say

I was sleepwalking a path to my dreams.

A pen and a pad; in my case, long walks headed nowhere like college first dates.

Now, don't get me wrong.

I love writing,

But I love sleeping, I wanted to sleep,

but it seemed like God was saying,

"Sleep not, my miss-guided servant.

Your work isn't finished.

I created the Heavens and the Stars

With words

Contribute to Creation

In one day.

Then Celebrated

The rest of night with the angels

Drinking drinks drowned from my Oceans

Unblemished

Rippling tidal waves

From my fingertip dipped

Clinging to a single drop of water.

Filling all 'A' through 'Z'

Including 'U' and 'I'

Made in my image, I know you can do more

Than just try.

Speak it, it's spoken into existence

For instance

I love you.

Love

That word is rumored to move mountains

And part seas

So you can see, who has walked with me

To the otherside.

Open up those eyes you have not died.

To the otherside

This is Why Kids Wanna Stay up Late

Of the table to kiss her when she's angry with you, because you love her.

To the otherside

Of a desk, In a classroom.

Teachers were students once

Still students in their classrooms

Learning while teaching

Because, they know the true meaning of stewardship.

To the otherside

Of the universe,

Because dreaming is boundless.

To the otherside

                    Of this page

                    Of this world

                    Of that pool

                    Of that track

                    Of your room.

Being disabled

Is more difficult than it sounds.

Even though

Contribute to Creation

They dis able

And do the impossible.

To the otherside

Of ourselves,

Because we all always know

We can be better.

To the otherside

Of the bank

While hell's army chases from behind

Attempting to remind and resurrect mistakes.

Regardless

Of the heart you've preciously placed

On every page."

And He went on to say,

"But, walk through hollow nights with me son

And Nothing

I mean nothing

Will hinder the words

That ooze through your pores

and rock your vocal cords.

If the words uplift one to safety,

One soul out of billions,

This is Why Kids Wanna Stay up Late

Let others recite their piece

Retain your peace and never cease

Until relief is given to all I've called."

Now, I'm in shock and awe.

Attempting to write,

And give an applause

It looks like I'm fumbling a football

And I call out,

"Slow down Lord.

I don't have enough time."

And it's funny, I didn't know.

Time

Is infinite and irrelevant

The past is sent by yesterday

Demonstrating what we could be creating tomorrow and the days that follow.

So get up and carry on, even if you feel like you're stuck sinking in sand bubbling sorrow.

You really wanna know what God told me

Without the poetry

and glamor behind the words?

He said,

Contribute to Creation

"Get your lazy behind up son,

It's time for life

and if it's worth giving, it's worth living."

Presented with what's true

I made a truce with the truth.

Because it's hard to swallow while choking on nonsense

Pussing empty promises.

So I'll acknowledge, won't embellish,

and allow God to tell this.

"Help those with less."

And not to eliminate the guilt in your heart

but to eliminate struggles you have the power to dissolve in the lives of others.

And pay attention thinking intangibly.

A man with everything may have lost it all to get it,

and a man with nothing may have given it all up

Including his heart, so others could thaw.

Look to the cross

It was for All, never None, old or young

We're flawed by nature.

Processing the process to progress as human beings

Cannot be foreseen within equations with the variables identified.

This is Why Kids Wanna Stay up Late

What we want

What we need

What we do.

What we want tempts us

What we need uplifts us

What we do defines us.

The definition written

Is a mirror image of how you're living.

Or lack thereof,

But as children, we knew pure love.

The color of your skin did not factor into friendships growing between mornings and streetlights.

At night, excitement was tugging at my soul like gold rush out west 1849

I was only 9 barely slept thinking while sleeping I was missing something.

I wanted to see

I wanted to see and I saw.

At night

There's stillness

A pause, throughout the chaos.

He woke me up

So I could rest in peace.

Still thinking insomnia?

Contribute to Creation

Never, I'm simply thanking Him for the gift He gave yesterday

Praying He gives me the same tomorrow

And the days that follow.

Even after death

Life.

Death To I

Your truest self, like had to be there humor, impossible to duplicate.

So to give respect to He who can create

Is a relationship we shouldn't attempt to fake.

Lost in a room full, it's a truth I can say,

but found like a newborn out the womb on the first day.

The Lord, Our God, provides all the power we need.

Believe be true breath new

To

See through

Former views before we heard the good news.

But with minds to move and hearts to sooth

I pray the pressure molds diamonds so I can drop gems.

Never sand but I am yet a man

Longing to belong and be different

Within the same breath that locomotes the hope pushing life through my veins.

Others hinder (t)His conquest as if they're celestial beings.

I assure you, life is not a contest despite what others may dream.

Never been one to compare or compete.

I let God cut my heart, with words silk sharp like a scalpel, then speak.

Is the message a reflection of me?

During quiet morning moments, God slays what I think.

No need for ink far from contemporary

Contribute to Creation

Poetry is the father-in-law, it was freedom that I married.

So styles vary from phrase to phrase, page to page.

I age, but the words I lay, will stay

One day to days, 2 months to years.

Let the food marinate then meditate.

It becomes clear

Like College Algebra with an answer sheet.

But the one for life was lost between order and chaos.

For anyone waking wishing they were laid off

Jump.

Arms spread like the crucifixion.

Not to fly but to die

Sacrifice is necessary for development.

If you want something bad enough,

You won't waste time to **rush it**.

Waiting for a Cataclysmic Crash

Blinking bricks, 3 a.m.

Normal people must rest easy.

My heart hungers for

Well, is it breakfast or still dinnertime?

Technically breakfast, but I can't break a fast I never started,

and eating after midnight isn't good for you.

Gaining weight sucks, unless you were me in high school.

My mind wonders and ponders precarious like political promises.

But within this insanity is where my honesty lives.

I am waiting.

For stars that never listened to their supernovas.

Unable to tread night.

Skydiving to enable wishes true.

"But aren't falling stars the visible path of a meteoroid as it enters the Earth's atmosphere?"

Says the Wikipedia jerk.

Thanks.

Knowledge at our fingertips

Now everyone's an expert.

Yet, illiterate to the excerpts our heartspeak.

If only there was an app for inner peace.

I Like to Make up Long Titles because I was Told not to in Grade School

True Story.

A little girl told me,

"When I grow up I wanna travel the world and give fresh water and food to eyes that never see it."

Questions crashed on the backs of my teeth, like thunder that knows your name.

Will that pay the bills? What do you know? Will it work? What are you trying to do? Who do you think you are?

Be an American girl, have a sweet 16 and smile next to your brand new car.

The art galleries of my heart opened throughout the cracks of my fingerprints,

and grew pictures of future fingers suffocating our pure past.

We cut our brake's throats,

and let our kid-hearts choke throttles.

While tongues never too young stimulate liquor bottles,

and Chris Angel pot-holes to pleasure.

Adolescent angels clip wings

Trading dreams for a mini dress and a cute drink.

No need for a brain

The self-deprecating lyrics will help me think.

While yesterday's righteousness; shimmering like a sunset seen behind prison bars

Wonders how it got this far.

This is Why Kids Wanna Stay up Late

This far from who we are.

This far from what we wanted to accomplish.

This far from what we wanted to be.

This far from what we wanted to represent.

This far from the thesis stating what our dreams meant to us.

If mirrors could not lie, vanity would not have a birthday.

Can ears swallow wisdom without listening?

Everyone is a Grownup.

Except for souls suffering from a mid-life crisis.

A generation dry-heaving genuine feelings.

Because before the age of four

Innocence was thrown-up through throats, like inner-city gang signs.

Coincidently, at the same time.

This little girl, pure as pirouetting moonlight on secluded lakes

Shared a dream with me.

Unafraid whether or not I approved or would accept it.

Only motivated by the music spinning like worlds

Within her heart's universe.

She asked, "What do you wanna be?"

I wanted to say, "A Poet."

But my fear said, "Famous."

SuperHuman

As a kid, we all wanted to be that superhero.

Super Sayian!

No, but yes .

I meant

"Super" saying

Meaning

Different from the rest.

There was more beneath, this obsolete

Identity implied.

To *fly*?

Arms stretch like humming birds singing

And gravity was defied.

Imaginations beating like humming bird hearts, and problems would subside into an abysmal

Nothingness.

Hell couldn't fathom.

Parents couldn't fathom.

Only God understands.

We should pay more attention.

In the beginning He created man, and we forgot how we began.

This is Why Kids Wanna Stay up Late

Now all I see is countless Hooks scraping strains of decency from our hearts

Urging us to scrutinize Peter Pans.

Look and listen.

The Lord is always looking to hold our hand

Like a father

Reaching Teaching

To cross streets only while He's around.

That image?

It's drowned like a fish flopping on the ground.

Going on quest for crowns

He's attempting to give us.

But we wish to live this privileged

Lavish

Lifestyle.

But be fooled not

Lifeisnotcopaceticbecauseit'sfabricated

With   fake

Smiles.

When I was a child.

Emotions were embraced.

I was,

Some would say,

Contribute to Creation

Socially inapt.

Unable to half-way emotions.

I wanted to be the image God projected on the walls of my heart.

But it's hard to figure out who you are and where you're going

While playing hopscotch with rocks in the dark.

Especially if our ribcages are glass houses.

Our self-perception's protection is not very promising.

If only vain critics could pick up picket signs and go on strike.

This poem is dedicated to the many ears told they would never write

Step behind the mic,

Or that they'd always be, children of the night.

Too bad life isn't a movie.

After every mistake,

There are no directors yelling cut like a knife castrating cancers we create.

Even though I believe the Bible is a script it's hard to get with just one take.

There are countless oceans of potential we can tap into

We are all meant to

Full-fill a purpose instilled at birth.

And like an Earth that won't spin, will you ignore what you're here for?

Are these vessels we call bodies empty corridors?

Will we socially reprimand propelling passion from our pores?

Like being who you are is doing too much if it's different.

Will you give birth to the hope you hold in our heart like the first scent of Spring.

Or trade in your dreams for the next cool thing like life is a video game store?

We are more than consumers,

and quantifiable numbers.

Our hearts hunger like a child's wonder

To release what lives under

This conveniently composed compilation of elements.

Irrelevant to our feeble or stone-chipped

Visual representations.

We check the TV like gasless service stations.

Dreaming to be full fooling our think tanks.

Now and never filled.

But don't fret or collect regrets

There's a pill for that.

But if you still don't know how to think, act, or feel,

And anxiety is latched to a lease of your life

Make sure you tune in tonight

You'll find great grade A advice.

How to keep up with a Kardashian, Be a Bad Girl, and if you're Leprechaun Lucky,

A Basketball Wife.

Or will you invite

The luminous lens of your iris to dandelion dance on the edges of your pores telescopes?

Contribute to Creation

Hear your heart's verses and see the many universes

Expanding infinite through your thoughts

Like your grandfather's wisdom giving life to a lighthouse for your future.

The fading beacon seeking your attention

Between the distance of your spirit and this human experience is not an alien.

There's a God inside you yet unconfined to

The limits we assign true.

Prayers spin the propellers pushing our dreams.

Speak into existence

The infinite power behind you.

(And ladies, not your glutes) I'm referring to the hymns spiraling from your grandmother's roots.

What is God Asking?

Trust.

Even when your hearts finger-tips tremble like train-tracks

While the red lights are flashing.

This is for the dreamers,

And the believers

Not just the critical poetry readers.

This is for the 3rd world prayers painting a path to Heaven

Van Gogh your woes and God will show His wonders.

For the lives around the world that need me, that need you, that need us

I need you.

This is Why Kids Wanna Stay up Late

This is for struggles never seen.

Little ones

You can bring this world to its knees with your voice.

Even when ears listen like lamps that lost their light

Speak electric like a love struck couple's chemistry.

Set your limits free

Bury them in a garden that never grows.

So you'll always know

At your lowest low

When it's darker than black

And critical lips claim, your rhymes are wack,

Or when you send hymns to Heaven, your voice cracks,

And that violin string you stroke doesn't sound so fresh.

Remember

We are all

Uniquely gifted.

You were never unequipped.

Our imminent death

Makes us

Superhuman.

Who wants to be a Kid gain?

I used to live in a mansion made of Lego.

And Lincoln Logs.

Dusty never dirty untainted unchanging

Memories, are clutched between star stricken fingers

Reaching for that light within darkness

Like fishing through impure pupils.

Shuffling salty sediments

Veiled by false sentiments

Searching

For something real.

Searching

For truth.

We will never learn to love

If our heart's ears are *~~mute~~.

This is a hearing aid.

Much needed nostalgia bursting through your walls like cherry Kool-Aid.

Too sweet and hyper active at times for iced tea lemonade stands slumberous summer days.

Unless you were a kid like me once,

and summer was a synonym

For over flowing excitement.

Like the first three rounds of a fight facing Mike Tyson.

This is Why Kids Wanna Stay up Late

Or the anticipation ducking behind your breath

Blowing through that flicking flame floating like a mother's touch above our birthday cake's icing.

We were one word from wishing,

and dreaming did not stop because you woke up.

You know what, this is before

Commercials coaxed our conscious comatose.

Before our dreams died drifting like ghost,

because that's when our kids, younger brothers, or sisters needed us most.

Before our hearts developed moats

Thwarting any boats of emotions,

because reality, like burdens, has a fatal attraction and reaction to gravity,

and grows thick-heavy like overeating, obese cinderblocks.

With hearts hard as rock,

Our lives have become too tangible to be touched.

Especially lost within this digital decade of text messaging-

LOL, OMG, reality TV, and Facebook.

Where everything is rushed-

Fast food, fast cars, fast women, fast living, and fast fads that pass

Quickly

Like fiber married to explosive diarrhea diapers.

Waiting to exhale, for the next update as if we were deep sea divers

It is time

Contribute to Creation

To let the truth swing free

Like windshield wipers wiping away all this bull fecal matter that never mattered and hold on to that something that something that mattered.

This is before how we truly felt was captured within the convoluted catacombs of common place conversations.

Your dreams are waiting by weigh stations where the world said your wishes were too much and that you weren't enough.

We are more

We are more than the weave we wear

The cars we drive

The make-up we hide behind,

and the expected roles we take on versus the aspirations we left behind.

This is before time was this Rock and Roll singer.

Sniffing his first snort.

Moring faster than the revolving doors tween the legs of a two dollar whore.

Her beautiful eyes

Singing hymns to home

Tattered by prayers.

Yet still, empty and unrevived like forgotten anniversaries.

A wondering withering guidance wishing to be young

And the young don't wish.

Only reaching

For more money

Fading, like childhood's heartbeat.

Muffled, like Spanish spoken beneath seas discovered and deciphered by Aborigines.

No entendemos.

We forgot to wear our smiles even when the lens cap to the camera is closed.

Our hearts auditorium is almost empty.

Empathy sits silent sleep in the back row.

Apathy, never made its way to the front door.

What do we stand for?

We college graduates and high school dropouts.

Equally unsure if we'll endure colossal criticisms written in blood

Scaring like glass.

We are struggling students,

and the teachers reaching with a hand made of marble

Glowing like morning

Forming a smile on a child revealing more teeth than a crocodile.

We are middle class parents praying our kids will be sensible.

We are single parent principals

Fingers festering full, birthing responsibility, hoisting failing kids up,

and unlocking hidden potentials.

We are God's incomprehensible science project.

Love was the hypothesis but we chose war instead.

We are the ribless walking dead searching for souls to complete us.

Contribute to Creation

We are the forgotten faces facing elimination finding home in the most humbling destinations.

Under bridges.

Park benches.

And the pavement.

As cold as hearts training eyes to transform us into glass and see through us.

We are here.

We are there

Riding hope on a voice rolling like a wave

Propelled from my sandbox friend.

Dribbling words upon hearts

Like hands beating drums

For the ones orbiting like moons around drums filled with fire

Sparked by old fliers.

We auction our lungs for cigarettes because breathing reminds us of the breath that navigated our nostrils.

Embedded like eternal fossils.

But our propensity to be docile

Dwindles like our birthday cake candle's last flicker.

We throw too much in the pitcher

Rushing to be the victor

And before we know it

This is Why Kids Wanna Stay up Late

Life moves quicker.

Stop.

There are lifetimes of joy between the seconds that die.

Permit your eyes to tango above Heaven's rooftop and salsa with stars drunk off moonshine.

Breathe deep like the oceans gasping grasping the emotions eroding the words we wish we could say,

The dreams we wish we could live,

The feelings we wish we could feel again,

and the thoughts we wish we could think.

Instead needles sink like ships into the icy rivers of our veins,

Lip cracks caress bottle caps.

Hungry hangovers devour hours that were once ours.

Take it back.

We are mountain movers, and breathing miracles.

From the whisper of His kiss we were made spiritual.

We are single mothers,

and lucky homeless retired vets

With 60 stories of sorrow lodged between our teeth, but society treats us as if our breath stinks.

No one listens.

No one hears.

We are waiters and waitresses

Waiting for the stars to fall like pregnant clouds.

Contribute to Creation

The sky is full, of clumsy kerosene kisses.

Our wishes are infinite. It's never been too difficult for the Lord to make your dreams come true.

The power is within you.

Our minds are more influential than viral societal sanctions that envy our uniqueness.

This is for everyone.

No one

Not a soul, is beneath this.

Help Those With Less

I was on South Beach.

The scene? Blue bottom breeze kissed by palm trees.

Muy hermosas damas.

Everywhere.

Todo el dia y toda la noche.

Despite the endless flocks of facelift females,

I met a man on these golden streets of decaying sunrays.

He said his name was God, and that He was homeless.

I asked this question.

"How can the architect of this universe not have a home on this Earth?"

Being God, He answered with a question and questioned my understanding.

He said, "Son, if home is where the heart is,

How can light live where the dark is?

And the soul can only receive

What the heart gives.

So, what you wish to receive, leave with me."

In an instant, I knew He gave Everything,

and my woman-chasing purpose was worthless.

I saw

As clear as a flat-line during a defibrillator's charge, that

My thoughts were resurrecting like hope holding determination.

The mission parameters

Contribute to Creation

Are as simple as easy-bake ovens, with a fixed mix, and a few brownies to cook,

or anxious fingers flipping through pages gazing at ancient figures in zoo books.

My soul is exposed like a church bulletin

Your choice to take a look.

Although the theme gets segmetized from time to time

The same pure true intentions should be kept in mind

Intertwined like distant lovers beating hearts of light.

Subduing the night, twinkling tickling the hope that lives within us all.

Listen.

I can't see the stars in their entirety,

but I know that they burn.

I'm not puking perpetually

Unceasingly nauseated,

but like drunken hula-hoops

I know the Earth turns.

And I'm not constantly immersed wrapped in extreme poverty

Yet, I am concerned.

This is for the lamps lost

Under adolescent lids that never burn.

And the stomachs that echo empty within classrooms

Still expected to learn.

For your nights unknown, and the family of 4 that feels more alone than an arid artic breeze.

This is Why Kids Wanna Stay up Late

This is for the scars of scripture on your knees, and the struggles we never see.

Because of the pride preventing your lips to push a plea.

Like a sick and shut-in's sunlight on a cloudless day; sometimes we must make a way.

Prayer isn't free, when you must scalpel your soul and pour parts of yourself to be heard.

For the voices never heard, this is for your words

Every syllable,

and every prayer for your plights to be livable.

The world may call you pitiful,

but I see an engine-full of light.

This is for every "umph!"

Just to make it through a double-shift night

So your child can choose the path for their life.

Sometimes only finding solace

In the celestial rewards our Lord has promised.

Single Mothers, Single Fathers

Your image of sacrifice should be admonished.

Even the eyes of impossible

Are astonished

At the task you accomplish.

Be inattentive to pompous politics

Expecting you to pull on nonexistent bootstraps

Contribute to Creation

Suck on sorrow like a pacifier until you swallow it.

But the first step is the one you take.

Educators

Cultivate the dreams within the hearts of our children and urge them to follow it.

Relevant to the path you create, it's irrevocably preposterous to the wages you make.

In America,

Over 15 million children live in poverty.

Convince me welfare ain't fair.

It's fine if you don't care,

but don't question the character of someone you know nothing about.

Of course the poor are looking for a hand out.

But this wish is not always monetarily motivated.

A hand out,   Reaching

Dipped beneath the breath of compassion.

Warm like a May morning.

Or a mother's smile after the worse day of your life.

At least you know, tomorrow will be

Better than the last, and the past is a shadow casted from the light you're looking forward to.

Step into it, familiar and unafraid like it leads home.

And remember

"If home is where the heart is

How can light live where the dark is?

And the soul can only receive what the heart gives.

So, what you wish to receive, leave with me."

If you want love, give love.

If you want compassion, give forgiveness.

If you want peace, give acceptance.

If you want to be understood, listen.

Please listen.

Like infants whispering secrets with their eyes

God is speaking to us.

And His people need us.

Battlefield Specialist

This is this is this is this is

For the prayer warriors.

Gentle shouts.

Heaven hear you.

No need for a sneeze if you grieve

Just believe, and God blesses

Always.

Sacred sentences slicing sorrow like swords of light.

Faith-filled pupils protruding from hopeful hearts

Guide us, toward the light.

Today, I will invite my uncertain sentiments,

because tonight we will not walk by sight.

Even when the white capping rugged waters are rough

Like Baltimore inner-city streets post-midnight

Take a plunge from the plank of plights

At any height.

Because man constructed advice

Can't compare to our Lord's insight.

What's a lifetime to eternity,

A second to a century?

Both are synonymous with our Lord's perspective.

But your thoughts, your cries, your prudent prayers

Your perpetual pleas to be free

Are never neglected or anonymous

Captured within the catacombs of our Lord's ears.

He hears your tears

They echo like bombs between His palms.

So remain calm

Never worry.

"But how do we cope in a cold world without a metaphorical coat?"

Simple.

Emanuel wrote the manual.

And if you're still feeling anxious, uneasy, & unsure

That's understandable.

But faith gives birth to sights seen

In our dreams we dreamt were intangible.

And if that cross on your back is feeling

Heavier than a handful of anvils,

Give God the handle

Bars.

His son bled redder than Mars

Rose like rose,

and closed the gates to fate deserved.

Contribute to Creation

We serve

The God who made this world with words.

Even when we feel as lonely as a minority in a 1920's suburb

His love

His love remains and reigns superb.

His hands reach out to the homeless cuddling curbs.

Seek to serve and deter the doubts dancing

Seductively.

Attempting to disturb

The message you just heard.

Speak like your words are wrecking balls.

Genocide barriers.

What are walls?

Every day is post 80's Berlin.

Come together, confess sin,

Release the chains that bind within.

Like Siamese halos

Repentance is change that never ends.

Are you sentenced to a cell of clever trends?

We tend to bend beliefs

When convenience collides with confrontation.

But fortitude is always easy.

Yeah, just like child birth with no sedatives.

Or watching the truth about yourself

Held between a reflection

Unedited.

No.

True Repentance?

Impossible without support.

Is the church a sinner's haven?

Or is it, just another place to behave and pretend

That our dresses and suits

Can mask the struggles that define us.

Pour prayer from your lips

Like hope dripping from a lighthouse,

and our Lord will find us.

Place the Lord on plus

And the flesh on minus.

I'm no mathematician but I believe the equation equals eternity.

Read and regurgitate His words

Within prayers, and let

Our Lord's voice linger in your mouth like gingivitis.

Contribute to Creation

Pray fortitude for the righteous

That they may never

Do what's right less.

Pray strength for the meek.

Do your part.

God to the rescue on cue, now you can fight less.

Pray perseverance to the dreamers, still flightless.

Pray comfort for the weeping seeking solace.

God will silence your sorrow

Like your problems ate too much

And got that itis.

Castrate idols

Search no more.

Everything we've ever needed

Resides inside us.

Jailbreak your words from your lips' prisons.

Those sacred sentences slicing sorrows like swords of light.

Silence your idol thoughts like a cold stethoscope.

Prayer warriors

Pray unceasingly

Connection never broken.

This is this is this is this is

My prayer

Amen.

Speaking Swahili to an American Moon

His prayer.

Grow a garden in my heart.

Be the stars that expel the dark.

Lead me to salvation like Heaven's sidewalk art.

Colors I've never seen.

Please convince sun-vomiting smiles to blossom between hell's hedges.

Our thirsty souls sip sweat smuggled from Your verses.

How do we unrehearse a curse conjured before birth?

Here's the bio.

13 year old men in search of water wells that work

Worth more than any treasure wastefully winking from this Earth.

Fitted in boots too big and a tattered t-shirt.

Fingers itching anxious antagonize A   K   4   7 bellies

Anticipating enemies who lurk.

And it gets worse.

The springs discovered beneath the Earth

Are contaminated from the surface soil dirt.

Due to the excrement left by livestock.

And I'm worried about problems I've got?

You know what it feels like?

This is Why Kids Wanna Stay up Late

Like I'm speaking Swahili to an American moon moon moon moon moon.

Is it possible to listen and never understand?

If understanding is listening, we must pluck our pride from the sand,

and adopt the ideology that shut mouths speak volumes

Like a deaf scholar signing a philosophy course.

It's hard to hear prayers while in love with the sound of your own satisfaction.

Can we love a world with words absent of able action?

But what can I do? What am I supposed to do? How can my existence make a difference?

Everyone is looking for a cause,

and scams breed behind them

Like a teenage Christian couple in love with lust afraid to trust patience.

We can give our time, money, smiles, and love to others.

Dry tears fall like bungee cords and jerk words from my throat provoked by poverty.

Obvious dichotomy should be an oddity.

But we would rather put our dollars in lotteries,

or TMZ Hollywood astronomy.

Children ranging in ages starve staring at a reflection of death and find their faces.

Silent tears float and freeze like comets.

Their remains remain unseen.

We sleepwalk and dream themes that deem their fate their faults

Our faults? Unseen.

Contribute to Creation

The mean doesn't matter. 1 life lost

Should leave our hearts distraught.

A toddler's body rots

While our bodies rock

To beats.

Seeking to sleep with the opposite sex.

We crease our slacks and buy a new dress or a vest to impress.

The possessions overcome us and we learn to love less.

Propelling our agendas while mothers and fathers bury their young

For the Earth to digest.

The images would be hard to digest

But a new season of "Real World" will help me think less.

Overactlive

I'm in debt, like everybody else.

I went to college

Accumulated this debt

So I could select

My future,

and not end up in dead ends

Like everybody else

Who didn't pay attention in High School.

I've lied to myself

On numerous occasions, like everybody else.

I need that new video game.

If I carry silence

Through these High School walls

Like a deaf newborn

It will ease the pain.

I love her, but my lower-half loves Every her.

I can change him if I try.

I know every minuscule detail

That trails the events that follow when I die.

Men don't cry.

When the odds are down there's no reason to try.

Children should follow in line and never ask why.

Contribute to Creation

I'll feel better in the end if I look into the mirror and lie like everybody else.

I'm always busy procrastinating,

Yet, I wanna leave a lasting mark on the world.

But how can I?

While riding on

Identical ideas of success.

More money and possessions than the Jones'.

I've lost myself

In moments of irrational purchasing patterns, like everybody else.

Fingers stretch reaching like infinity's promises grasping for guidance hidden within darkness.

Purest light sits majestic and marvelous,

but even streetlights drown out stars.

We can't pay attention to everybody else.

My truest intentions are to give my gifts,

and enrich the lives of everybody else.

I'm complicated, complex, and capable of change like everybody else.

I say, "I can't judge."

To justify the hypocrisy my lips give birth to.

If only, I could give it up for adoption.

Maybe I care too much.

That's what a girl said to me during High School when I wrote her a poem.

A wise womanizer trigger-leaked the secret like a church gossip sniper

This is Why Kids Wanna Stay up Late

Women crave attention never given.

Now everything is "just kidding."

Sardonic sentiments are intimate with our innocents.

Urging us, to mimic the synthetic security

Rippling on the retinas of everybody else.

Why do we grasp so tightly to what's not real.

Someone shares a truth on their heart and we forget how to feel.

If our heartspeaks, like foreign films without subtitled reels,

Do we even know what we're telling ourselves?

Is this path we walk ours?

Are the hours of dedication worth it?

If everybody else could care less about the origins of our Lord's winds

Propelling the sails of our souls like we were meant for more

More than touch and go thoughts that breathe brief

Like dreams

Auctioning their wings for unneeded comforts and pleasures.

Or halo hymn humming voices touched by God that never sing.

Flood Release fear like your heart's levies broke.

I pray the waves come crashing like an infant's smiles.

Even if you feel like you're hiking Calvary's blood beaten half mile

Swallow your tears like truth, trails nourish faith like fertilizer.

If our character's candle light

Was never dimmed by the whirlwind

Contribute to Creation

Of tomorrow's uncertainty

The garden of yesterday's dreams would grow tombstones.

For those feeling most alone within crowded rooms

Everybody else

Desires that devotion it denounces.

And will attempt to rip ounces away

That made a way for the path you built with blood, sweat, and tears.

Like God's promises, remain true.

Be you.

May you never falter, forgetting your child-like passions and fascinations.

Well, we haven't

Because everybody else is a figment of our imaginations.

Shadow of the Saints

I am the voiceless.

Soul-deaf, never speaking simply making noises.

I am, your poor judgment.

Resent me

Yes

Consequently, I am your bad choices.

I am your ex-wife or your ex-husband.

I am that fear you felt

Feeling, you could never really trust him.

The gardens of my pale nights grow sin.

I am never open to any negotiable notions of love's irrational emotions.

I write it off as nonsensical commotion.

I am alone

Like wandering waves wishing for a shore to call home

In the middle of the Pacific Ocean.

I am the kickball kid never chosen.

I am the playground bully's abusive past never spoken.

Mouth eternally open, perpetually pouring poisons.

Equipped with lie loving lips that love to speak of God's glorious wonders

But, I will never know Him,

because my heart knows no hymns

I am the unknown end

Contribute to Creation

To chaos undisturbed.

I am the black educated mind's justified use of the "N" word.

Even though I've heard, of Emmitt Till,

and other southern blacks who have been killed.

Executed lynched up by their limbs burnt to a crisp undeserved.

Therefore, my empathy was born dead, never resuscitated.

My *heart's* at rest, never defibrillated.

My chest beats mute hymns to the loced out low brim unchosen.

I only know winter, artic atriums, blood flows frozen.

I am life within the rush to the grim reaper's touch.

I am the ignorance that ignores the librarian's hush.

I am in the back of your classrooms.

Never quiet or compliant constantly defiant.

I am the lying lawyers and their guilty clients.

I am the dwarfs blade-walking on the shoulders of a giant.

The spotlight is the enemy I yearn to touch.

Nobody can get higher than I am

I am the pinnacle of perfection, I need no correction.

I am all over the place with my brief contradictory beliefs

Yet, I am headed in no direction.

I am the results of the year 2000 presidential election.

All hale Bush.

I am the corrupt officer of the law blowing on that Kush.

This is Why Kids Wanna Stay up Late

Arresting young black males who sell the same dimebags I inhale.

My truths, are the remains of the castrated conscience.

Shadows of the light searching for sun,

but never find it.

Blinded by deceiving diamonds

Preaching false findings, licked from the lips of a void-wish.

I am the sneaker to sneaker violence.

Unnecessary conflicts never avoided.

Positivity pushes like a locomotive

But with empathy eroded and apathy activated, you can ask

"Where is the love?"

And I'll gladly answer.

It was eradicated.

Innocence impregnated, by the jaded joust of jealousy.

Negative negotiations embellish me.

I am the reflection we all fail to see.

Unsee me?

You'll inhale my hells and your morning meditation's exhales will impale your derailed purity.

I am the virgin's reluctant first time.

And yet, the pornographic images you secretly see, mirror me.

I am

The denied existence of your insecurities.

Contribute to Creation

There's a reason small children find fear in me.

I am hypocrisy.

I am the Tupac Westside till I die wanna be.

I bring death to your community.

But I'm what the streets wanna see and wanna be.

I am you I am me

I am never free from a culture that defines me.

Lost in the same box the idiot box boxed me in is where you'll find me.

I only mimic mindless messages that are sent to me.

My gods are BET and MTV.

My loose lips speak with authority

While I lack understanding.

I found the true image of a black woman

On Vh1 reality TV programming.

I am a basketball wife.

Your guilty pleasures.

The worst version of yourself.

The secrets no one knows.

I am a leech

I am hate.

I am heartless.

I am, your Darkness.

"The Candle's Blue Breath" pen sketch by Samuel Hawkins

Part 2 The Candle's Blue Breath

Surpassing death and disease; articulating your personal secrets, innermost ideas, or simply standing in front of a crowd runs through the ranks and sits at number one when it comes to fears. When I was a child, after church my family would congregate at my grandparent's residence. I was so shy. Some Sundays I'd stay in the car and pray I wouldn't have to speak when I ventured inside, because eventually I had to partake in the Sunday dinner. My grandmother, like most southern black grandmothers, is no stranger to the inner workings of her kitchen. To say the least, she knew what she was doing and could throw down. My appetite would override my fear when I smelled cornbread.

Despite this popular paralyzing fear of presenting and speaking in front of groups, it is now a passion I can't picture myself **not doing**. I believe that God has placed a passion below the soils of all our hearts. The seed planted may be completely contrary to what you expected, but once you uncover the identity of what's growing within the garden of your dreams, a crossroad is born. We are all uniquely gifted. Even those of us who share similar talents have personalized accents to add to our craft.

Once we find the flame that simmers the passion we possess it is necessary that we feed the flame. Good thing none of us have responsibilities and life is always simple like quantum physics, rubrics cubes, falling in love, and filing taxes. In the unceasingly rapid rate in which time passes, we'll discover distractions and the all too popular preference to conform to complacency. Why are we in a rush to quench our insatiable thirst to hedonistically create? "I was always good at…" or "I always wanted to…" are phrases that illustrate an indication that we've relinquished talents birthing passions paving paths to futures meant to be, but choices make the difference like sugar in southern sweet tea. What will you choose?

Whether you paint, rap, write, recite, sculpt, build, act, or draw it's your choice to cultivate that passion growing below the garden of your heart. Will you stem oxygen to the candle holding the flame begging to burn blue? Please don't misunderstand. My **intentions are not to reprimand or erect guilt and** regret within anyone's heart **who** doesn't pursue passion to the maximum degree. I'm asking everyone to be aware of the existence of our innate desire to contribute to creation.

Upon discovering this need to leave behind something beautiful is a choice. Will you suffocate the fire or feed the flame glowing from your heart? I'm suggesting we venture down this path of discovery waiting for us like sun-famished horizons. It is never too late. Even if you have a demanding job, a spouse, a family, or other positive stresses in your life, you can still be conscience to the fact that you have something to give this world. Frankly, I have no clue what it is. It may be a picture, a poem, a book, a song, a symphony, a portrait, a toe-walk, a pop, a lock, 16 bars, or a dress. If you so choose to rip this gift from your heart's safe I implore you to burn blue and give us something beautiful, something magnificent, something moving, something accessible, something personal, something honest, something true, something new, something. Even if a world won't listen or won't see you, I humbly thank you for your contribution. Don't be afraid of the light inside you.

This is for those who are afraid of heights

I'm not looking for mountains to climb.

Get too high

The perception of reality is altered

Footing falters.

Thoughts cross like time and space created between the worlds

Generated

To distance ourselves further.

Sentiments secrete like sweat from unfaithful sex saying

"You know what? I've done better than "most" best.

No need to confess feelings, calling tenderly to the altar.

Stumbling fumbling over mistakes wouldn't be proper.

Why bother?

I'll make peace with myself and God tomorrow."

Like we know we have more time to borrow.

Diamond encased watches watch time just the same

As wood stain hour glasses filled with white sand

So understand me when I say

I'm not looking for mountains to climb.

The world can keep its hidden treasures

Lost within the imagination of its own heart.

This is Why Kids Wanna Stay up Late

Nor am I set apart.

I am a confused reflection

Staring back at the world

Finger fixated on me, I alone struggle with my impurities

So why would I suggest someone to mirror me.

I rather you forget me,

and remember these words.

I too, am in need of amnesty.

I feel that we should all be on a perpetual path to perfection of what we plan to be.

We all are. We're here. We exist.

But there's much more we can be.

Your library of linguistics may have been bended and amended within the same sentence,

but I know you understand me.

I don't flick my wrist to write fancy.

I fancy your true feelings so that we might intertwine as delectable as licorice,

and find some type of spiritual healing.

Because we all need a nudge through oblivion when knuckles cry red,

and our legs have lost feeling.

Yes, blessed with burdens gifts neglected or cultivated are double edged swords we are wielding.

You are either destroying or building the character of those who surround you.

Despite our culture individualistic ethos

Contribute to Creation

You have subtle control of what those around you amount to.

So, before your grip slips through the slits of my palms,

Close your eyes and count to infinity.

Yes, my intentions are to uplift you, but that was meant for me.

I'll close my eyes, too. Hold on tight and insist we fear not

The mountain we see before us.

Faith.

Faith the size of fist

Can shift tectonic plates

Conjure an earthquake,

and disintegrate any obstruction that used to exist.

Now mere myth, a whisper on a tongue, a shadow telling stories in a back alley.

Persistent rivers can make mountains into valleys.

And persistent humans can make memories into what we can do.

From the darkness it is a hand that I hand you.

Struggle is something we all do, but never plan to.

So let the Lord plant you in His garden. Unharden your heart and pardon yourself from self-propelled obligations.

We gorge on goal chasing,

and forget to love.

Forgetting to look within, we condemn

Believing everyone should believe what we believe right now,

and we don't take the time to love.

This is Why Kids Wanna Stay up Late

Wondering if we left the stove on

On the way to church

While we forgot the love on the stove cooking

Roberta and Mr. Hathaway are still looking

For another answer to

The question

Where is the love, besides?

Me Me Me, or I I I

Trying to get higher than the next,

But be fooled not

There is another path to select.

I not looking to go up or around I'm going straight through.

I'm a **mountain mover with nothing to prove.**

I'm not looking for mountains to climb.

Get too high, lose sight of little things.

Like granny's cooking and that moth ball smell lingering on clothing like childhood calling long distance.

Don't forget where you're from.

Don't forget how you started.

Don't forget you were a kid once

With a world uncharted, and a conscience that couldn't be bartered by senseless quests.

A world offering more while inward growth grows less.

It's okay if you're afraid of heights.

I am too.

I am too.

This is for those who feel being vertically challenged is inadequacy

Nocturnal notes float like helium kissed dreams followed by ruby words glowing white,

Like 6 year souls Christmas day

Finger-flick keyboards illuminate the room like bulimic window shades

Throwing up sun-rays.

It's been said

The lowly are with God.

So in this country,

Why do you think we sing old Negro spirituals from the bowels of our guts on Sunday?

So swing low, like chariots.

Pick up your cross daily with vice-grip fingertips shaking contagious, and carry it.

And tell your old life to have a conversation with a 12-gauge face to face

And bury it.

Beneath the sand you used to stand.

Sometimes we look back at life,

and can't quite understand,

"How can there only be one set of footprints?

How?"

Our human rationàl can't make it make sense,

but I'll tell you this-

Contribute to Creation

For the Lord to flow through you...

No, like totally through you.

Through every nook, cranny, crevice, and orifice

Of your body,

You must be vacant.

For the Lord to flow through you

Like moon-lit waterfalls moonwalking down valleys

You must be vacant.

Because eventually, like sunsets dying into darkness,

Every knee will bow, and the proud will feel as lowly as hell's basement.

Lost and locked within

Your past

No future

Only questions

No answers

And time.

Time to wonder where all your precious days went.

And because our lives are not cell phone plans,

No roll-over Minutes.

One second behind the past is ancient.

And moments?

Yes, the sweet moments reverberate through history,

and affect our legacy.

A life absent of God has no efficacy.

Self-sacrifice daily within my adolescents

Was a feat from my father I was blessed to see.

Giving relentlessly without interval,

Is an integral ingredient to love's recipe.

And Jesus gave His life.

(So we could live)

But the 3rd day

He rose

And got higher than

Saturn's satellites lost in Heaven's trajectory.

So, our brother being crucified may epitomize what Socrates was attempting to theorize.

Except, he drank hemlock,

but still we must remain locked like dreads

Dead to ourselves.

Put your lives on the shelf,

and remain connected like 4 with our Lord on one accord

Even if the water's whitecaps get chaotic we cannot jump overboard.

Trails and temptations are opportune chances to spiritually grow

So, like 1998 Tickle-Me-Elmo's

We must be sold out.

No compromise,

Contribute to Creation

None.

But don't get it twisted

Like a neck tie cutting off circulation causing hallucinations.

This was

Never for me.

Never.

The lowly are with God.

Those willing to debase to see His face.

The lowly are with God.

More frequent than the panting breath

Pushing through the airways of an Olympic swimmer's chest.

I thank my Father for my father.

Providing everything I needed, plus his time.

He taught me how to play catch and throw a football

Instead of looking for mountains to climb.

Why, climbing mountains

Deters attention and deteriorates fatigued faith.

The path is narrow and straight

Move mountains and glide gracefully across lakes.

Have faith.

And get low like limbo or face spiritual limbo,

and when I say get low

I mean drop it.

This is Why Kids Wanna Stay up Late

And when I say drop it

I mean your pride, ladies not your backside.

So throw the sexual innuendo out the window.

And move steady and slow.

Allow your nose to make love to a rose, eyes still closed hands connected

Keep counting.

I have secrets I need to tell you

Hidden deep within the caverns of my fingernails

Next to my boogers.

And yeah, whatever, it's out there.

I pick my nose when I don't think anybody is looking,

but what do you do

When

You don't think anybody is looking?

There is no light, within darkness.

Therefore, no gymnast sunsets back flipping colors

From the grave

Making Bob Ross, fluffy fro and all, marvel at its majesty.

Within light

Where there are actual facts to see,

and no such thing as blasphemy.

Within darkness

The only beauty

Contribute to Creation

Is contorted.

Like baby remains, after its aborted.

Yet some of us cling to the insidious image

As if it's God's graces and adore it.

And while the rush at first may seem euphoric

All these worldly idols will leave you stoic at best

So give it a rest,

because eventually

The self-exalted will echo lonely

Like playground gunshots, searching for home

Like Amelia Earhart.

Peer within your heart, and find what's at the center.

As if its been hiding on the side of a milk carton.

And I certainly care less than a degenerate father

What any critic has to holler.

Any present right now?

Sink further back into your seats

Don't even bother.

Because I am here

For the Father.

And he's not the center of your life

You're rolling dice with your afterlife.

The Lord only knows chance in one context.

The many given while you're living.

The glory?

It's not hidden.

It's down to Earth, deep within its crust.

Full circle back to where we started-

We were made from dust.

We must learn to trust,

and know this dreamcalledlifeisnotarush.

The lowly are with God.

How tall are you?

X

The Lord is near you.

We all have hidden hurts

Even though we may not appear to.

Eyes lie, time is truth,

It eventually comes out.

Just listen

I don't sleep much.

Fascinated with the night stargazer,

Coupled with procrastination what am I truly chasing?

An imagination without insulation

I can't hold back

Like an infant's infinite impatience.

But like everybody else I've got to be patient

Because I've got more worries and bills

Than a chronically ill hospital patient.

But the struggle illustrated

Keeps me motivated

And writing out of this world

Like space stations,

and ancient star constellations

Tracing shapes staring at me

Before gestation.

But I've been waiting waking

Aching to get this right

Like I'm adjacent.

Because sometimes I have more pride than the Puerto Rican Nation

At a boxing competition

But I listen

Contribute to Creation

Most of the time.

Most of my time listening.

I hear

I hear

That everyone wants to be heard

Like prophets' premonitions,

and women's intuition spoken with perfect diction

Every little one's every little word mentioned.

Fear not

Don't be afraid to fall in love with your art.

Although, I've been poked in the heart by a few rogue spears bleeding redder than reddest red

Like my grandfather's hands

Blood ridden from Cotton picking but still driven.

Right now, it's time for submission.

Like 3 and 7 undivided your attention

As if you're a toddler using a urinal

Susceptible to missing

The point coming across like

Refugees, Country to Country

On their knees

Praying to God for needs,

and new knees to ease the swelling,

and some may feel like foreign immigrant issues

Aren't worth telling.

But my other side assures me

I'll write what's right if I write from the heart.

And I'll have Her confidence

As long as I stay confident.

Whether or not I'm an outcast

Or in the mix like consonants

Her love is constant and it's beautiful being able to love when you've been lied to more than a Fox News correspondent.

But it's in the past, so I'm beyond it.

And neither side of my love is proud

So don't call it cocky.

But I can write stairways to the Heavens

Words dressed in tutus on the top dancing like Rocky.

I'm not here to pass a test, or meet a standard,

or be this cynical hypocritical over analytical

Claiming to be innovated entertainer

Reusing the same material.

But you don't hear me though.

I

could

care

Contribute to Creation

less

if my

Stanzas   or   structure   to   you   may   seem sloppy,
guesswhat. (?)

You can't stop me.

I'm simply expressing myself

Let the kids express themselves

I want the kids to express themselves

The arts are essential to a child's development.

Empower the youth with a voice like wolves serenading moonlit midnights.

Drunk, drinking hope Like Tomorrow is promised.

Thank God it never was.

Today would decay like

Creativity cradled within the desolate crevices of factory gray walls.

Good thing money is everything.

Tell that to a soul that knows death.

If we knew what was next,

I wonder if faith would be hard to collect.

If Tomorrow isn't Promised

Do me a favor.

And hold love close

Take a toke of joy,

Then like hippies huffing hemp, man.

Make sure you pass that

Next, transform into an aristocrat,

and give a toast to your existence.

Be glad you're here.

Breast cancer thought it took my aunt

She merely went home.

Yet still

Now you know.

24/7 like sleeping eights 8's

Hearts ache and break for love ones lost.

Within the cosmos

We are the mumbling murmur of the morning mist.

And you, are powerful.

So when you're gone

Make sure you'll be missed.

But before you leave

Let go of every fear hiding beneath beds begging to be noticed.

Even if your heart's fingers tremble

Contribute to Creation

Like a black man's hands during a not so routine traffic stop by a racist cop trying to keep everyone honest.

Yeah, Right.

Let go

Of every inhibition that said you were incapable.

You are able

To do anything,

and nothing

Is impossible.

However implausible it may seem.

So even if you have to

With your eyes wide like the Texas sky during day

Don't be afraid to dream

Huge.

Like my Father's hands when I was a child.

Each finger was a world,

and those imperfect palms reeking

Of swing-shift held me and my siblings up

Like galaxies suspended within space cradled by the universe.

So for what it's worth

To all the parents out there

And my Pops,

I'm sorry for booking that ticket to Know-it-all-Ville when I was a teenager.

This is Why Kids Wanna Stay up Late

The day we become know-it-alls

We know nothing.

So before you move your mouth like a jig generated from a 1953 speakeasy

Take your time, think it through, and speak easy.

We won't always know everything about what everything means,

and what does that exactly mean?

Belief,

In anything

God or yourself

Without faith

Is like a honeymoon without whip cream.

It just can't happen.

So maybe some things are impossible.

Like a life without her, or a life without him,

Or maybe it's just illogical.

But even for the big bang to be explained

It took an ounce of faith to retain the respect that it gained.

So when I look up into the Heavens, and find peace within His presence

It shouldn't seem that strange.

Honest question number one.

With this precious life

As fragile, yet more powerful

Than a pistols bullet propelling pin,

Contribute to Creation

Which direction should we aim?

Eradicate third world hunger pains,

or watch idiots boxed in the idiot box?

Vicariously voyaging on their passions pursuing

Fortunes glitz glamour and

Fame.

But not for doing anything.

Famous for being famous is an aimless pursuit

To pulverize our own right to personal peace

Like ravenous beast

Why do we ferociously feast on attention like High School class clowns
wondering, why?

Why is what I am within not good enough?

Will I ever be good enough?

Will I ever be good enough for this World to accept?

If I answered your request

My assessment would be incorrect.

I suggest,

Look beyond your own reflection and be better than what you expect.

Because in retrospect,

Nobody remembers what they expected of you in the first place.

Because when the music fades, and the lights dim, and the fads change,

and the frantic roar of the crowd wanes into an abysmal nothingness

This is Why Kids Wanna Stay up Late

Only your thoughts remain.

So before we leave ourselves willfully constrained,

Fearing history will forget our names.

Do yourself a favor and let go

Of everything,

and give God lingering loads.

Stay in tune with the Holy Spirit instead of going rogue.

Splice out isolation, Christ is waiting like premarital sex Christian couples praying positively for a negative sign,

or menstruation.

That's my story.

So, my spiritual aviation is marked by crash landings

Disciplined deceived disintegrated any chance of understanding.

But the Lord's words of wisdom are uncanny.

Even when it's been a harder-knock life than Annie.

Your testimonies My testimonies Our testimonies can lift others and plant seeds.

God gives gifts and the increase, so cease to fancy the faith constructed by man-made presidents.

We should want everyone to be Heaven's resident.

No goal no soul is ever irrelevant.

When our patience with others is prevalent,

Our inner-peace is under development.

Find love

Contribute to Creation

Relish it

embellish it with more fellowship.

Rip your chest open and embroider it on your heart's chambers.

Pray to Him and say to Him

Lord,

Give me the holy finger

Versus

That other one I wanna use when that rude motorist cuts me off in traffic.

Purge me from the urge we, often fall victim to.

Help us listen to, that whisper within winds inclined to find our hearts.

Pierce the pulse like nihilistic needles

Crumbling our social constructs.

Find the face of God and be love-struck

Like smitten children carving names within notebooks.

Take a breath, of fresh love,

The air as soft as an angel's sigh,

and let it pirouette roses within your veins swirling peace like the eye of a hurricane.

Like scholastic all-star fingers crowbarring books, open your mouth.

No praise is vain if we are spiritually trained.

His heart is always open like summer-day windows.

The feat we do every morning of waking up, He is instrumental.

For every breathe beating beneath the wings of our hearts

This is Why Kids Wanna Stay up Late

He is instrumental.

His voice births music in my ears,

I guess you can call Him instrumental.

Sowing sweet words in our souls tastier than fudge-sundae eating utensils.

Despite the horrors you've been through, His love is more monumental.

The life He gave you should be a rental.

Because the task He's asking is quite simple

Follow.

Because if tomorrow isn't promised

We don't have time to doubt like Thomas.

If tomorrow isn't promised

What should we truly admonish?

If tomorrow isn't promised why are we running from life and waiting for death?

Because Paul said it in Romans 8:31,

"If God be for us

Who can be against us?"

Lower your guard down

Show no resistance.

You have been granted permission

To listen

To your heart.

The Voices in my Head need Affordable Housing

I'm crazy.

I hear voices.

They tell me things.

But from the mouth of a text book

Regurgitating some kind of clinical terminology probably, no.

Nonetheless, I couldn't afford therapy.

Like most kids where I was from

I was broke.

I had no money.

Financially dead, I picked up a dream and a notebook and wrote poetry instead.

Still there was a need to alleviate

Voices bouncing around in head like cerebral wrecking balls.

Wrecking all that was not pure.

Erecting walls within hearts

Piercing skin protruding through limbs dancing on winds like daisy stems.

My phlegm, is mortar quartering pictures attempting to be painted like Porter.

For voices dissecting destinies

With freezer frame hearts.

It's difficult like choosing Cold Stone combinations or Christian denominations

Passions dwindle,

Perro es calienta, call it south of the border

Hablo un poco,

90

but never a no show.

You can see the passion when the vain in my throat shows.

I hope these words grow

Fingers reaching stretching

Squeezing hearts

The way other winged-words

Mimicking angel-aviation have touched mine.

So let me tell you what they told me when they touched me.

And not like that.

I know what you're thinking,

and it's inappropriate.

Here's what they told me.

Open your soul to worlds undiscovered

Dancing through cracks of your fingers

Like it's a middle school sock hop.

Get lost in forever like a broken stop watch.

Stop and watch

The sun rise like dust,

and at dusk

Let it reflect and glaze down your eyes like fresh water from a spring in an obscure forest.

Contribute to Creation

Search where adventure is

Where the wild things are

As if you have golden locks testing porridge.

Immerse yourself in nature like you forgot to pay your mortgage.

Trust me, within this life you have more than you need, you can afford it.

And always speak with passion, until your voice grows hoarse.

And of course the passionate source will reinforce the torch burning blue within your throat.

Words spoke, laced with dope.

Let "want"

Survey the sentences the syllables are haunting

"Middle class families are living on the streets?"

Daunting diction inflicting societal friction

Minds insisting wishing fiction,

but the conviction within the description convinces most to listen

Listen

For those who didn't make it to this page.

Eyes that graciously gaze

Go grab their ears,

Propelling phrases

Puncturing rupturing eardrums

Until a message is conveyed

This is Why Kids Wanna Stay up Late

"Yo, you don't know what you're missing"

We've been missing

We've

Been missing

Their faces, their stories, theirs songs.

Their triumphs, theirs hurts, their humanness, their loneliness, their desperation.

The voices in my head have already said they need affordable housing

They're homeless.

The voices in my head said they need fresh water, their wells are toxic.

The voices in my head said they need

Fresh food, their ribs are showing like a typical model.

So, I guess for being lazy we could extradite them all to LA

Where that's socially acceptable.

Then there wouldn't be a problem, right?

Wrong.

The voices in my head said that they need us.

They need us to be free.

But that freedom can only be ascertained by paying with a liberating loneliness.

A willingness, to stand alone like mountain peaks speaking a language

We always knew, never learned but forgot.

Love

Contribute to Creation

Pure and unfiltered.

I'm sure if Jesus returned right now,

Floating like fallen leaves,

He wouldn't be conservative or conventional.

We've gotten caught up with percentages.

Desensitized to the images.

We live our censored lives above their crimson cries.

3rd world and next door lives swirl distorted like a hurricane hell.

It's an endless ride.

Until we reach with a hand soaking soggy dripping love.

Hidden City

Sidewalk sleepers could be abundantly warm if stigma was a heater.

Yes, justice is blind in our country.

So tell me, should the blind serve as leaders?

Invisible men slip through cracks stolen by the grim reaper.

Deinstitutionalization induces the situation promoting alienation.

Administered from big wigs of our administration's nation,

We're taught to see hoboes and hate them.

But the lowly are with God, we should exalt them.

Humility has been castrated, harassed, and hated.

Paraded on videos as fools for our amusement,

Handed segregated sentences, labeled as a nuisance.

Eyes clouded with consumption serves one function.

Serve the satisfaction of your self-willed purpose, even if it's worthless.

Jewels, cars, cash, and clothes

Is human life worth less?

Strolling the strip of South Beach,

Masculine eyes fornicate with women they meet.

While permanent pavement pedestrians, viewed less than men

Travel on flightless hope, searching through trash for eats.

For weeks they weep while we seek more idols that induces our spiritual defeat.

Eyes open, veiled by want/ We don't see.

Contribute to Creation

Lost souls with no last resort/ We don't see.

They were kids once, dreaming miracles/ We don't see.

Eyes fixated on fancy cars shining like stars/ We don't see.

Pimped by plasma screens, They remain unseen/ We don't see.

We don't see/ We don't see/ We don't see.

No, we won't see; a person in an unfavorable predicament.

We judge the homeless like our lives defecate innocence.

While our capacity to love dwindles limited.

Therefore ungodly, God is love and love is infinite.

Any lingering variables are an insignificant, at best impotent, attempt to make sense of it.

"Homeless People got money!" Nonetheless less than you & I.

If we deprive the lowly, our souls will surely die.

So may our hearts break like the teeth of a plastic rake.

Open your heart's gate and let love overflow for the world's woe.

Especially for those below our American totem pole.

Be bold.

Go against what you've been told until all stories are told.

To genuinely help someone is more valuable than silver or gold.

Unplace your plans from pedestals, cease to pass them and trap them (between the cracks)

Instead ask them, What do you need?

I am here to serve you, your cries caressed the ears of God, and I heard you."

Rest your heavy heart, love is forever fertile bearing fruit.

Help Those With Less.

An interesting sentiment. Can one love without love dripping from their pores? Unending comfort is a conundrum whose sum equals spiritual discomfort. Why do we fun so much and upside-down frown artificial lenses? Why don't we smile-hope mirrors and recover reflections of God? Are mission trips to give or receive? If we come back to the same dream, did we ever leave? Houses hungering for nothing, grieve and have hearts missing something. When you have it all, you lose everything. When you lose everything, God is visible. Ah! To lose is to gain to gain is to lose. "Now relinquish your possessions and follow me." Most of us refuse. Who wouldn't want to take a cruise, shoot pool, look cool, and wear wool over lies and swallow luck like delicious magic? Giving has nothing to do with money except everything, we own is sown to the seams of our souls. Embrace your lows and moments of doubt. Give and listen with pure hearts.

Struggle Cleft

Sing a song for the broken, the voiceless and the hopeless.

The isolated, roaming alone childhoods decapitated

Therefore sightless.

Faceless futures; flightless and faithless.

Poverty stricken predicaments are ageless.

Piercing pupils sever confidence like guillotines.

Hearts cold stiff stuck like steel beams.

For some, morning never comes like broken clocks.

Then we turn our vision

Away from the television like

Hips hungry for hip-hop.

While our eyes unwatch struggles that never stop.

Just because the commercial ended doesn't mean the struggle is over.

And while we sing this to the dreamless

Erase the unnamed from the struggle-never seen list.

Is poverty and profitability seamless?

Or can we afford to give more to the poor?

Now, money isn't meaningless,

but your time, energy, and love-

Are more valuable than a Genie's wish.

You can save a life with a sentence

if your Empathy stays strenuous.

This is Why Kids Wanna Stay up Late

Stretch your words like ligaments-

and give gifts of acknowledgement and time to families suffocating beneath struggle- not a myth- living it.

Hearts' of the innocent will not benefit

From love leaking loosely and stubbornly indolent.

Forsake forlorn statistics.

Even if it's an isolated incident (heartspeak) listen soft;

I saw. a 9 year old boy

Carefully packing his school lunch for home.

The other children?

Eraser-teeth/ empty chicken bones.

I asked,

"Why didn't you eat?

You're not hungry?"

He responded,

"My next meal, unknown,

and my little sister's cries

Make my stomach's groans

Grow guilty like OJ and Anthony lips."

My lips went silent like the 5th on Chappelle,

and gave goosebumps until my skin was basketball brail.

And spelled this poem.

Contribute to Creation

"The less we possess-

The more we give."

Hungry hearts dry-heave chains.

What we devour

Returns like a lie, full grown as a religion.

What truths have we been swallowing?

What moronic myths have we been following?

And what values are we borrowing?

Take everything give nothing?

Infinitely wanting?

Whether the full is filled

Overflowing

Like gasoline suns sucking straws

Connected to cups (gurgling) kerosene.

A brother's sister eats lullabies for dinner.

Should we intervene?

Or does life go on.

Is this Darwin's dream?

Are the rest of us just strong?

Naturally selected?

Poor ghetto kids

Neglected

Must be infected

With a disease that leaves

Their souls defective.

Instead of food and water-

Let's roll through poverty

Clutching the wheel of a Lexus.

This will impress the kids-

Provide a fresh perspective-

And illustrate where America's respect lives.

The present and the pursuit of possessions.

The "Now."

What is future? = Our children.

But "empire building" called shotgun

Destination-

Lower overhead.

"Get Yours" with a Middle Finger to a bleak world

Is the legend that we *wed*.

But before we throw the bouquet

Or even kiss the bride to be-

Look inside your eyes and see.

Yes,

More times than never-

Life isn't fair,

Contribute to Creation

but like rectangles and squares,

Our differences can't compare

To familiar traits we share.

Before we lost love

Looking

Elsewhere for acceptance

Accepting we are spiritually impaired.

Untrue

Like lucrative lotto promises.

Am I American or lucky?

Like a Russian orphan's abdomen bleeding beats from a xylophone rib cage.

Hear the homeless

Hear the broken Beats that seek our eardrums

Hear the young ones

Hear that song for the broken your heart-sings.

Mother Marie, fornicate the law,

and give mute hearts an abortion.

Awaken silence.

Hear the song for the broken ringing.

Ringing like doorbells on a brick house cemented by prayers never heard drowned by coveted success we never found.

Hear,

Their song.

God is with You

I speak marathons.

Like, pregnant hormonal Women

Lost between walls at a hair salon

Gossiping about nothing

But everything.

And like everyone else

I dream.

But rarely do I dream dream.

Sleep, eyes closed, unexposed to worldly woes.

The rafters are blinding

Everything is binding

I can't tell the last from the first row.

But that's good right?

Lord is light.

Only He knows, next direction I'll go

So, like broken treadmills

I'll keep walking

Faithfully

A willing probe.

Praying I won't stub another toe.

All that we must know

We're simply supposed to supply more souls to the gate.

This is Why Kids Wanna Stay up Late

And this is the reason why kids wanna stay up late.

Tears roll down cheeks and fall up like prayers

In desperate attempts to negotiate.

In a world made with a love so great,

How can we generate so much hate?

I wonder if it's a

Legitimate debate,

or am I simply ranting the semantics of Human traits.

But then we catch a glimpse of the beauty

Between the ugliness and death,

and we learn to appreciate.

So while you concentrate and comprehend

Do me a favor.

Ponder bliss while I admonish this.

If we're conscienceless to our astonishment

Of toys, trinkets, money, power,

Designer dresses worn by Designer women,

Cristal, crystal balls reflecting our

Loneliness like stars flickering sound language.

But no one listens, and language is dead without attention

Therefore you're

Killing the voice of the child within

That use to speak and line your lips.

Contribute to Creation

Someone said

"Shhh, don't do that. Don't be bold for God. You'll never be good enough to live up to His standards, so why try?"

Suckered out of your soul and your goals

Your insides are ripped,

and you decide to quit.

That's why I never,

No, not never,

Tell a child they can't take on the world,

because they can.

As a kid, I was addicted to the truth.

Therefore, more of a man

Not afraid to cry, not afraid to die, and not afraid to ask why and admit

I didn't know the answers

To the many questions playing Dodgeball within my neuro-pathways.

As clueless as a critic

Ranking a masterpiece.

So, why don't we let old young you,

and old young me

Keep stretching on like a morning yawn.

Waiting reaching for the kiss of dawn.

Praying for the patience and spirit of a pawn in its place drowning in faith.

When the speech is spoken

This is Why Kids Wanna Stay up Late

Peep the notion, open your ears like a broken suit case.

We are not here, to appease the pupils of outside confirmation.

Trust me when I say,

Desires will dissolve when your own interpretation jeopardizes the operation

Which is salvation.

The Lord's love is   Constant

It goes on forever.

We create the altercation

His words need no alteration.

Taste it.

It's an awesome sensation.

If you are lost and waiting, His call is stating,

That we are all created,

In His image.

Fingerprints

And Unearthly scents resonate radioactively

When we search actively, and tactfully, we are practically, fractional portions of the people we actually could be.

So stand up, and straighten your legs like a closet homosexual.

Repentance is here, to ensure all lives are correctable.

In fact I

Am a former fornicator

Veiled by monogamy.

Contribute to Creation

But the Dichotomy

Broke the threshold and push forth honesty.

Honestly,

I idolized my relationship and worshipped sex.

I was confused and lost as if I was taking a calculus test.

But now my faculties rest, on the crucifix

Swinging from necks like pendulums resting on most of your chest.

Like an "X" marking the spot

Give God your treasure chest.

It's like playing Russian roulette with a full clip

Commit suicide daily then resurrect.

Reborn like butterfly

Inject patience it's not time for that kind of pleasure yet.

Better yet, crumble to Love's humble mumble

While hate entangles in its own over exalting fate.

He from his own throat letting his name reign

Will be devoured by his echo

Deliverer of his own pain.

Speak with a firm hand of gentleness.

As if it holds an infant's neck.

And let peace protrude from your tongue like an ice sickle from Heaven trickling into madness.

Dangerous yet delicate.

This is Why Kids Wanna Stay up Late

Celibate fingernails forgot what dirt was

Skeletons not only reside in closets.

They walk among us.

Soulless shells seeking solace.

Empty eyes mimicking midnight.

While we ignore the healing hand of our Lord

As He offers to give sight.

Reevaluate your intentions, do you even wanna live right?

From music videos, to a kid's television show.

The world demands our attention.

Lengthy poem, long-winded I know like Chicago winds blowing bellows

I speak marathons but I listen lifetimes

To the life and the times of the people

The people who were told hope was myth and faith was fantasy.

Shun profane and vain babblings.

God is with you.

Razor-blade fingertips dipped in death

Contemplating suicide,

God is with you.

Syringe-stain veins injecting pain who forgot His name

God is with you.

Powerless people be patient,

His hand will reach you and this time will teach you

Contribute to Creation

The Lord is always with you.

This is for the lost and lonely souls.

Just looking for a way out.

Lives like labyrinths it's hard to imagine it.

Lost within these twist and tangles of your own life.

I hope these words

Irons out the creases and leaves your heart in pieces,

because it's not about poetry or sounding profound.

We're simply supposed to supply more souls to the gate.

And annihilate the hate.

Because where there's love

That sweet forgiving forgetting everything you've ever done love,

God is with you.

God is with you.

God is with you.

God is with you.

God, guide us with you.

Sunshine Shenanigans

Be the antique music-box locked between unborn Siamese dreams tearing at my soul's seams.

Peripheral passion to poetry

Harvest my heart's dreams.

Open up that mouth like a mute scream.

Sing Spring

Sprout doves

Sweat love

Like bullets pulled from the trigger of monogamy.

Wait for me faithfully like Penelope.

I'll chase like Odysseus,

and we will call this

Pendulum pursuit, the sequel to the Odyssey.

Then because you're a women

Naturally

Find the kitchen, make me a turkey sandwich and don't bother me.

Just kidding.

But seriously, I want roast beef.

Still joking but for real

Lets hit the road like Bonny and Clyde.

Keep the theme of highway robbery.

Except for currency,

Contribute to Creation

We'll steal hate from the hurt hearts

Of troubled souls of this world,

and replace it with the laughter of little boys and little girls.

Let's repaint this Earth the color of new beginnings.

With the same brush

Instantly illustrate your interest.

I'll pay a premium principal of attention and add interest,

but just one more favor before I sign this waiver

Regarding our conversation's contractual agreement.

Section D paragraph 3 within the fine print,

and I will personally,

Yes, personally delineate the documents in case you can't find it.

"When it's the 4th quarter, Cowboys are playing, 3 seconds left, 4th and inches.

Wait until the game is over and I'm required to be interested."

Ok, it ended.

I'm listening, ears open like first date car doors I need more

Spill it out like your ribs are fire.

My thoughts are quarantined to the song your heart sings.

Can my name be the chorus?

Because you've been running through my thoughts like Forest.

Let's go kick it like Chuck Norris.

Take a hike to Heaven's Hills and watch the glowing golden moon rise like the birth of god.

Check your inside like surgery and find affection for me.

And let's avoid questions that place me in the position of perjury, for example.

"Does this dress make me look-?"

Let me tell you what I do see.

Your smile is a poem that never ends.

Like a fuse burning backwards at both ends it looks like a semi-circle searching for its soulmate.

Shimmering silver like the crescent sailboat moon that never thins.

And just because you're not a "loser" doesn't mean you can't win.

That's our little inside joke, tell your friends not to ask.

But I digress, back to the task.

My lady, if you were the worst gift this world had to present

It's a sure bet, hand up quicker than the class pet.

Voluntarily, I'd come in last, if life was a race.

And if life was a race, you'd be the finish line.

And I'm purposefully oblivious to the many masculine heads shaking back and forth like metronomes

As if saying something sweet is a senseless crime.

This is a poem born from nights lonelier than Hollywood hearts.

If your life was a motion picture

Only something as beautiful as my Grandmother's wisdom could audition for your part.

My heart has questions, be the answers.

Every day with you is like breath after being diagnosed with cancer.

Better than the last/ looking forward to the next.

If my affection wrote a book

Your Name

Would grace every page within its index.

Fun

Please

Don't not believe the ways the world has concocted.

They are

All lies

No truth

The essence of deceit.

See me

I was tampering toe to toe with temptation alone

The essence of defeat.

You can't compete.

I tried, and they died.

Fathers, mothers, brothers, sisters, aunts, uncles, 1st, 2nd, 3rd, and far off cousins, nieces and nephews will wear black, suffer, and cry because of me,

and the Paul, Remy, and McCarty that was in my system.

Nevertheless; their relatives will miss them, because I hit them, I fell victim

To my own flaws,

and I knew it was against the law to operate an automotive vehicle when intoxicated

But I did it, and can't negate it.

Hours ago, I was enthused celebrating because I made it

Out of high school, but I was a fool who didn't listen to lectures pertaining to

DUI's.

Contribute to Creation

See, my teachers tried, but it was ineffective.

Now my life is much like my Lexus, destroyed.

EMT's firefighters and the boys in blue deployed.

My scholarship to school?

Identical to the Old Testament law

Null and void.

But you can learn from it.

But for what?

For what reason, will a whole family

Grieve and need compassion and support?

They'll get their "Justice" in court.

But for what?

I had it all, but under age consumption of alcohol was the downfall.

Otherwise known as

Fun.

The term used by my peers frequently.

Now that you see where it leads to, you still wanna get a drink with me?

I'll probably get Four counts of vehicular man-slaughter, now what do you think of me?

In the passenger seat was Janice

She was an engineer.

Behind her was her son Adam

He was an athlete.

This is Why Kids Wanna Stay up Late

Beside him in the backseat was Nina.

She wanted to be a nurse.

At the wheel was her father Paul.

He was physician.

They were on Elm and 44th with a green light, he couldn't avoid the collision.

88 too fast to pick up in your peripheral-vision.

There was no way I was missing, when I reached the intersection.

They were wise enough to have on protection.

But it made no difference that all four of their seatbelts were strapped.

It was a side impact.

Hit and flipped that Cadillac Escalade 6 times until it laid still on its back, lit up like match, smoking like a factory stack.

I listened for the screams, but no screams only charcoaled bodies to extract.

Now the EMT's have me on my back. Trying to tell me relax,

But I can't,

because I know time, can only move forward and not back, and I have to face the fact

that my one mishap

has left 4 lines...

Flat.

Step across the Line

For anyone

Who has ever been encrypted with the classification less than human,

Or

From lackadaisical lips labeled

A Loser.

With a life linked to an existence of playing catch with words,

flung like bullets, from mouths mimicking missile silos

on impact igniting exploding on eardrums like nuclear warheads.

Never,

No baby, no never

Forgetting

The words said

Until dead

Heavy harden hearts

Lined with lead.

Before you give up or give in

Come on,

Step across this line instead.

Fragile,

Flower stem finger souls

With more weight

To carry, within this world than a child should ever have to hold

Step across this line.

You are not alone

Unremember

The rhetoric

Reprimanding your aspirations

Lingering like wrist written lacerations

Even if, your self-confidence is

E vaporating,

From constant attempted cyber-bully assassinations.

Your survival within these hallway worlds is fascinating.

Keep

Your deepest dreams, desires, and goals

Locked within your heart's locker.

Away from everyone else.

Especially yourself.

It may be hard to admit it

But like Simon's lips,

Reflections are the worst critics.

Dream destroyers and destiny determiners

Reverence is irrelevant.

Contribute to Creation

Hold on

Don't let go

To that God glow beautiful smile

Cracking the center of our hearts

Like loves quaking; soul shaking; epicenter.

And for those

Shivering souls

Not for the environment

But going green, developing this sickening hue, breathing blue, colder than bottoms of winter's shoes

Step across this line.

For any alienated angels looking for your wings in all the wrong places,

Step across this line.

Cut and pasted faces laced with hatred

Step across this line.

Bad day bullies face-fisting peers

Fearing exposing the woes enclosed in closets

Buried In graveyards of acceptance

Step across this line.

If you've ever been singled out for being too much

Or being too "good" or not good enough,

Step across this line.

If your parents are divorced, and it sent your heart north

Frozen like the feelings you've never expressed,

Step across this line.

If the mirror is an adversary you spar with daily,

Step across this line.

If you've thought this world would be better off without you

Without your accent,

Without your uniqueness,

Without your contributions to creation,

Like your life was something the rest of us could afford wasting,

Wrong.

Step across this line.

If you don't think anyone understands,

Step across this line.

Contribute to Creation

If you're hoping someone notices the bruises you Halloween-hide with make-up,

Step across this line.

If you're being someone you're not,

Step across this line.

If you think you're alone,

Step across this line.

If you miss her, if you miss him,

If you're hoping the cancer stays in remission,

It you're missing a Man who was never your Father,

Step across this line.

If you want to give this world Something,

Step across this line.

Limp across this line.

Crawl across this line.

We need you.

"Quenched Starlight" mixed media by Samuel Hawkins

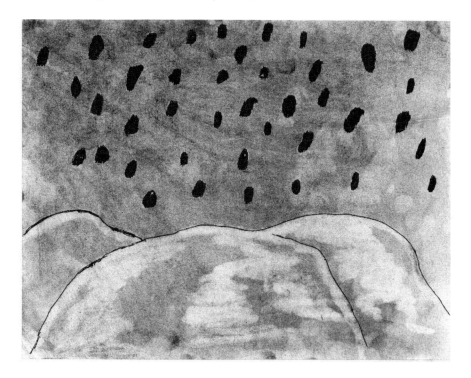

Part 3 Quenched Starlight (midday)

eyond the depths of despair and darkness is light. Time is a blessing, beautiful or torrential, nothing between our breaths last forever. Lost within the looks of a lover one would request for more time. Even the unfaltering brilliance of sun will pass away. Moments die, if you're familiar with the aroma of struggle you're probably thinking, thank God. Hold on, even if there's nothing to hold because the light dancing within your soul forever-glows regardless if you know. Art is an outlet; show this shimmer. I write to encourage and implore the implication of any art-form chamber-locked in your soul. Your light is waiting for a trigger to dam-lock release darkness, so we can see you. I want to see, and the world beckons, too. One of the most beautiful sights to see is someone perform a task they were made for.

What are you made for? What are you? Are you a picture of your pain or a visual representation of your perseverance? Have you ever seen an eagle fly after its wing has been broken? Why does this inspire us? Flying is what it was made to do, and there have been countless eagles before it that have flown with problems of the sort to deal with. We appreciate the eagle's triumph because we see ourselves within its struggle. Life is not easy to tread and everyone doesn't make it this far or the next day. When it all ends, none of us make it. What reflections will you leave behind? After the death of every moment we define our life. What song will ring when we play your track? I hope it's a love song.

Like birth, at our darkest and most inconceivable moments we shine. Survivors of sexual assault, physical, and verbal abuse humble my crosses to splinters when I hear a testimony. To overcome, forgive, and move forward after experiencing the worse side of humanity is a miracle in motion. I marvel at the mechanics it takes to forgive. I can't half-way forgive myself sometimes. When we can let our past die, it bursts like a sea of dandelions to bloom a future that smells just like hope. We can only hope for what we don't have. So, hopefully hope stays stuck in the past and we can see our faith take flight even if its wings have been confiscated by doubt. Struggles don't taste as bad as "Lifestyles of the Rich and Famous" suggest. Struggles are hearing aids to catch the rhythms God note-knocks to our eardrums. It's hard to hear while gnawing on words and images of death connected to hooks leading our spirits to a slaughter we could avoid if we'd listen.

We listen. But what do we listen to? When black people embrace being "niggas" and women embrace being "bitches," it's like breaking into prisons we're trying to escape from. The most popular and insisted advice usually isn't the wisest. I've done time in this prison of "Peer Enforced traits." There is nothing common about you except the hope to be more than what you were yesterday. Hold this hope like it's your last breath and exhale faith until you find the forevers hiding between the moments when life is at its heaviest.

We are celestial bodies. We carry those crosses so we'll have fire wood when the world river-swallows our fires to smoke. Inspiration is a spark. Someone is draped in darkness. Take your creativity out of park and give something genuine from your heart. Not a high-class luxury, all of us need art.

I'm Tired

The night is yours.

This night, is ours.

This is for all of the abuse.

For every black eye, and every loose tooth.

This goes out to all

Of the tired souls more exhausted than my grandmother's hands.

Lives dysfunctional disarray spinning out of control like a broken bolted ceiling fan.

Confidence crippled shaking unsturdy like a redwood without roots.

Shivering submissive from men mimicking myth swinging for the fences with an iron fist

As if their name was Babe Ruth.

Lives lost and filled with more fear

Than a suicide bomber unsure of the truth staring down the barrel of a M4 held by an American troop.

This goes out to all

Of the busted lips

Caressed by crimson kissed finger tips

Reaching

For light.

Holding on for dear life.

Stubborn eyes, locked behind lids, replay the rape that was recorded last night.

So don't ask me

This is Why Kids Wanna Stay up Late

Why I write.

Don't ask me, why I fight.

Don't ask me, why I recite.

Don't ask me

When less than 50% of women in the court room receive justice.

Don't ask me

Why my tears sing a song of sorrow praying for a better tomorrow.

Don't ask me

Why I speak up and out.

It's time for all of us

All of us

To loosen our lips, and take them off mute.

And give the entire Psychological perception of femininity

A reboot.

And make sure every "victim"

No, Survivor

Sees victory and that they always know

They are never forgotten

Like rotten fruit

Once beautiful

Still beautiful

No

More beautiful.

Contribute to Creation

We should look up to you like mountain peaks kissing clouds.

Your eyes shine hope

Like sea-sick stars throwing up the way home.

An ugly situation, can give others restoration.

And I know some of you out there are praying that you'll never have to reveal what's underneath.

That you can keep your secrets, hidden between your tongue and your teeth.

Let me tell you this.

Every time you speak your grief

You give others relief,

and make the crosses I have to bare in my life

Lighter than a leaf dancing on the wind, like Beethoven's notes.

Hear it and feel it from the back of my throat.

I am tired

Of seeing smiles hide behind clouds like lonely moons

Bathing beneath icy tears,

Bottom lips trembling terrible

Dribbling drops of fear.

Hope is here,

and you, ain't gotta cry alone no more.

Hands welded together like cast iron bridges bonded by the brush stroke of God.

We caught

This is Why Kids Wanna Stay up Late

Your shrieking whispers withering from your heart

Limping like lost limbs

As fragile as a lilly's stem

Bended like a hat's brim

Scratching at my soul like lost voices

I hear you I hear you.

I hear your pleas

I hear your "Stops."

I heard your "No."

And I hear your screams

Waking night like domestic fights,

or bed bug bites.

In spite of your plights and many sights you've seen,

Let's not forget the ongoing theme.

Think Red and go Green

Think Red and go Green

Think Red and go Green

Think Red and go Green

Think Red for the blood that has been shed,

and go Green for a future

That is more serene.

Somewhere someone is suffering, and that bothers me.

Somewhere someone feels unsafe, and that bothers me.

Somewhere someone believes nobody will believe them, and that bothers me.

Somewhere someone feels all alone with no hope to hold on to, and that bothers me.

Somewhere someone is gazing through a mirror and hates what they see because they blame themselves, and that bothers me.

Somewhere someone

Stands mausoleum mute still

Confined to a bathtub

Scrubbing skin but the stains will not come off, and that bothers me.

And it should bother you, too.

This

Is for all the abuse.

For every childhood stolen and family that's been broken.

If you ever forget the way home

Look up to the stars

And know

Every night

I'm crying out to them

for You.

And while you're on this Earth

You are never

Alone.

Collateral Damage

This is for every child

Who grew up as a carcass.

Perfect pupils, penetrated by darkness.

Practicing prayers

Those sweet prayers

Lost between lips, trapped behind lids.

Tip-toeing through minefields that used to be playgrounds.

Vietnamese children, raped by American War heroes.

Bathing in Agent Orange, to souvenir the sorrows.

Reaching for their severed limbs standing stoically still.

Sight

Swirling white

Like the barrel of a bursting gun.

Bodies

Infested by

Bullet holes

Blazing red like the rising sun.

Were these forgotten daughters and sons not meant to have fun?

Were they not meant to soak and absorb beauty like an adolescent sponge?

Or a righteous root searching for truth, desperate to bare fruit?

Were they not meant to get messy like a finger painted masterpiece?

Contribute to Creation

Or make mistakes and negotiate unsentimental parental mandates for staying out too late on their first date?

Why, is everything made with pure love always engulfed by hate?

Were they not meant to be great?

Were they not meant to be anything?

Were they ever anything?

Did they ever mean anything to anyone or are they nothing?

And if they are nothing

What are we?

What are we doing?

And where,

Where are we going?

And what's the future showing?

Where are we heading?

With all that's going on, what are we getting?

Except more money.

More of our mother's tears falling like anvils on Jupiter

More   Memorials.

More coveted precious metals.

More monuments to remind us of Him.

To remind us of Her.

To remind us of caskets kissing folded flag creases.

This is Why Kids Wanna Stay up Late

To remind us of pieces of ourselves forever missing.

But she still waits.

She waits for his return.

She waits like an orphan's eyes piercing through windows wondering when...when will this empty tomb tormenting her thoughts like flashes from the paparazzi pestering Nagasaki survivors. Tear drops fall like mortars,

Memories jerk her flesh like bullets,

Finger-tips touch a tombstone, only a name remains.

7 months pregnant not even premature labor can trump her pain.

Her husband was a soldier.

She is a widow, soon to be single mother.

How many lives were lost when that RPG bursted like Heaven's destruction.

How many lives are lost when weapon manufacturing contracts insist perpetual production?

How many more lives are lost when we submit to war's seductions?

Her insides churn like 5000 ancient eruptions under Earth.

Each pore, a volcano spewing anguish.

She would give every lifeless possession just to change this,

but political agendas are numb to empathy and

Deaf hearts speak the strangest language when trying to vanquish foes.

Fear, hate, and war breed accordingly.

So of course we see this

Viscous cycle swirling distorted like broken back ballerinas.

Contribute to Creation

No one survives a war.

Give me my son back

Give me my daughter back.

Give me my sister back.

Give me my brother back.

Give me my mother back.

Give me my father back.

Give me my best friend back.

Give me my cousin back.

Give me my uncle back.

Give me my aunt back.

Give me my innocence back.

Give me my husband back.

Give me my wife back.

Give me my life back, but you can't.

We strut around like gods until it's time to make a miracle.

God's Forgiveness

I wanna be born again.

Resurrect me yes, God.

Fine tune the violin within my throat I don't wanna sing this sheet music anymore.

Wake me from nightmares.

Send me a dream in the form of a drink so I can toast to a new existence.

Swallowed; by darkness, fear, hatred, and resentment

I wanted to end it.

My temple was thirsty for the round resting like autumn's leaves within the gun chamber but you subdued my anger.

Now God's forgiveness lives here

Between barricades, resisting rage, rumbling my ribcage

Like rock swallowing thunder, under my sternum's stage

Below the bellows, where my organ's orchestras used to play.

Yeah, we should have called the song "Swallowing Grenades"

I died inside that day.

But God's,

Yes God's forgiveness lives here.

Beneath the pugnacious rusted roots of my heart

My story starts and my childhood stops.

Father like familiar hands frisk like 1991 southern California cops.

Only 9 years of age, with more luggage than the LAX airport parking lot.

Contribute to Creation

Powerless, and why speak to ears severely immune to the words

That hurts, please stop.

That hurts, please stop.

That hurts, please stop

I don't wanna do this anymore.

That hurts, please stop

Where is my mother?

That hurts, please stop

I want my father.

That hurts, please stop

I don't wanna do this anymore.

That hurts, stop

Where are the heroes, the heroines?

The Genies

With their wishes,

and fairytale beginnings?

Just stop.

My voice was the only voice there to listen so I just stop

Speaking,

and it's hard to pray with no words to say.

Curses and laments alike ripped from my lips as if my voice went on strike from the unwelcomed invites but

God's forgiveness lives here.

This is Why Kids Wanna Stay up Late

Releasing

Pain from the past is a path that intercedes with the seeds of forgiveness.

When we resist this,

The mistrusted thieves deceived by greed, power, and domination leave us

Winless.

It is impossible to fight night with darkness,

Fire with flames,

or hate against hate.

It negates the peace

We're all trying to administrate, **but get it straight,**

Having peace does not require a requisite of passivity when it comes to sexual assault of any type.

Whether it be verbal or physical

Neither is minuscule.

So, whether you're at the workplace, college, or middle school

Utilize your vocal tools.

Learn that your lips are defibrillators. You can save a life with a sentence.

And never again move your mouth lackadaisically until your words sprout like Heaven's daisies propelled by peace piercing this atmosphere,

and have no fear

There are voices behind you that support you

Just report truth and those voices will grow ears and never ignore you.

So after this poem sees its last sunset

Contribute to Creation

Turn to your mirror and turn your tongue off silent as if it's a cell phone leaving church,

but right now, give it a moment of silence for those who hurt.

I hear you.

Please hear them.

The night is being painted red with voices we should recognize

Please hear them.

Please hear them.

This is for the shattered souls

Lonelier than AM interstates.

This is for the court dates

The rapes and lives they disintegrate.

This is for the families and the tears reflecting like diamond lakes.

This is for the delicate flower fingers shaking like earthquakes.

Tongues telling testimonies.

You inspire me.

This is for the panic attacks and the childhoods we can never get back.

This is pity for the pedophiles and rapist

Living life loveless.

This is for trust.

This is for the lies and broken promises.

This is for trusting again.

This is where the suffering ends.

The night is being painted red with voices we should recognize

Please hear them.

Please believe them.

Please receive them.

Please see them for who they truly are.

Where are the heroes and heroines?

When a survivor can unsilence the shame,

They stand right before you.

Despite your tambourine tongue

Shaking uneasy like the unsure dreams of children,

I can see the Lord's forgiveness

Building a building around the pain you've been concealing,

Wielding your voice.

The night is being painted red with voices we should recognize,

Please...

Rise

Your heart's voice

Is sea.

Rolling these thoughts like moonshine tugging tides

Rise.

Like praying hands calling falling stars from the other side.

Finding nullified lullabies

Buried beneath, a church basement.

Burning breathing flames

Swirling the signatures of four little girls names.

Slain, September 15th 1963

But not in vain.

Mistaken martyrs a part of

A necessary picture.

So young ladies

Think twice before you think you have to take suggestive Facebook pictures

Posted tagged

Half naked to make it.

Innocence taken

Soul vacant

Heart breaking

Into pieces

Release this

This is Why Kids Wanna Stay up Late

Popular persona

Of the

Video girl

Haunting your insecurities of what you truly aspire to be like a pestering poltergeist.

My advice, stop shaking like dice and speaking up like mice,

and don't you forget

Don't you ever forget

The names of those who weren't given the dignity to be coerced, but rather, were forced to sacrificed, but you are beautiful and you should embrace that.

The pucker of your lips and the curve of your hips could transfix the eye of time.

But you

Black women, are perpetually powerful

When you utilize your minds.

So rise

Like an 1864 southern summer sun.

Yanking a sometimes weary but gracious morning.

Mimicking your angelic fingertips

Birthing the son of freedom

Warm burning beautiful and bright.

You bittersweet color of coffee and of night.

Your pupils, your beautiful pupils

Carry constellations for

Contribute to Creation

Shackled slaves searching southern trenches.

Surviving, ash-stricken Earth southern lynches.

Longing liberty's lingering withering finger pointing

Northward

Toward glory's destination.

And yet

Post emancipation, we are still facing

Segregation, within our nation's

Oh so sufficient "No child left behind" kiss my black behind style of education.

Advance placement courses reinforces and further endorses the separation within race in relation to the socio economic status and strata of minority families.

And for those who haven't navigated their neurons through sociology 101 and can't quite understand me, or don't want to,

Quite frankly,

We need to challenge all of our children

And make sure that all of our children

Are wielding

The proper reading and comprehensive tools conducive to their grade level.

We are quick to quarrel over seas and watch our children bleed before we teach them how to read?

But I can see you.

Like I can see

This is Why Kids Wanna Stay up Late

Harriet Tubman, with her revolver and her stars guiding her.

I can see you

With your pens, your pencils, and your teachers leading this future.

So dream huge,

and tell this world to make room,

and show it why the caged cannery carries a tune like Maya Angelou

And sing me home.

Addie Mae Collins

Carole Robertson

Cynthia Wesley

Denise McNair

Sing me home.

Nikki Giovanni

Sing me home.

Gwendolyn Brooks

Sing me home.

Coretta Scott King

Sing me home.

Zora Neale Hurston

Sing me home.

Billie Holiday

Sing me home.

Rosa Parks

Contribute to Creation

Sing me home.

Etta James

Ella Fitzgerald

And Aretha Franklin

Queen of soul

Sing me home.

Because your heart's voice is sea

Rolling these thoughts

Like that moonshine

Tugging tides

Don't be afraid

To tell these little girls

To rise.

Rippling Sunshine

An epic history

Muddled with misery

Caressed by visions of victory not all eyes are alive to see

From

The senseless, unrecorded on the census spousal induced injuries to the words of Maya Angelou rising like dust within the resurrected ribcages and spirits of men, Women and Children provided everlasting energy.

Words

Opening hearts like morning curtains casting light on this nation's

Many atrocities burning beneath the embers of infamy.

Unsparingly spoken from the shadow-laced lips of femininity's

Enemies.

And not just what the sociological text books say, "Rich white men."

Like most minorities

This self-deprecated disrespect is derived from an internal entity when you ignore responsibility.

And drown your dreams beneath the reach of your ambition's distillery.

Brewing beauty

Castrating complacency

Cultivating confidence

Through the hallways of your radiate seeds

Buried beneath soils of your soul

Begging for birth

Contribute to Creation

Anxious to rise above the Earth of your eyes

Like wildflowers

Clutching the skeletal remains of an abandoned factory.

Whispering the secrets history forgot.

Do you not know from whence ye came?

Ladies,

It does not take physical chains to constrain your liberties.

Your voice gives birth to a choice to choose your identity.

So, swivel your thoughts and pay attention to the taught tendencies of the social media industry.

You are more than the size of your mammary glands.

You are women

So naturally you think and reason in mystic methods. As a man, I will never truly understand, but you can still have ambition.

You can still have dreams.

Or you can choose not to.

But the speed in which you can make your gluteus maximus move does not mark your maximum potential. This is not the most essential credential you are meant to cling to and embrace.

Before you leave the page, let me leave you with this question.

Would you add brush strokes to a masterpiece?

It doesn't matter how much make-up you plaster to your face or how much weave you wear in your hair. What you look like on the outside has nothing to do with being beautiful.

That mirror

Reflecting an image viewed as truth, cannot give an accurate depiction of who you are.

And, that voice whispering darkness behind your future's lips suggesting seductive sentiments encouraging incongruence body modifications

Irrelevant to this benevolent beauty God hides and seeks within soul, is not yours. That voice is not yours.

You always were and will always be

Good enough.

Never unworthy.

Never below the expectations of greatness.

Never less

Do more.

When an unforgiving world threatens to omit your dreams and implode your wells of shimmering wishes

Be allergic to "No!"

It was always yes.

Catch vertigo high hopes as if it's a fresh start for the first time.

Imagine infinite.

Anything is possible if you can illustrate the image in your mind.

Your existence is necessary and miraculous.

You were meant to be and I can see

Your grandmother's grandmother smiling a sunrise above your dreams' horizons.

So before you shake your tail feathers like male peacocks while the beat rocks

Contribute to Creation

Stop

And ask this question.

Who

Are you gratifying?

Who

Are you satisfying?

The voices that curse your existence?

Or the voices that lifted you, that gifted you,

Infinite opportunities by means of sacrifice and undying persistence?

Will you listen to their voices or will you pull triggers executing a respect women have died for?

Because your past is on her knees like a pre-executed Jew praying Holocaust horrors on her lips.

Begging that you will remember her.

Will you remember her?

Or will you pull triggers executing a respect women have died for.

Because your history is not barren like the breath of yesterday's broken promises

Limping through lungs, wheezing withering songs unsung.

Like starving children

Mouths were open

Voices pleading

Souls were bleeding

Hearts exploding through arid throats like the birth of a sun, and like a trigger-less gun

Lips were made deaf.

And still to this day

Young girls disappear within the realms of the sex trade.

This daily violence, invokes a tear-swallowing silence.

Women have become a global commodity.

And it's a huge problem if it just bothers me.

This poem isn't just for the "ladies."

This is for the fathers and the fathers to be.

Can you see, those tired arms reaching, beating the gates of a glass ceiling?

Climbing a ladder, absent of rungs until the battle is won.

But sorrow is not the song that I hear

Victim is not the image that appears within the echoes of my eyes.

I see light, rippling like halos held together by faith.

Ms. Anthony I hear you.

Ms. Angelou I hear you.

Ms. King I hear you.

Ms. Chisholm I hear you.

Ms. Dickson through your pages of poetry I hear you

Ms. Earhart through the air I hear you.

Ms. Frank through a generation of hate I hear you.

Ms. Roosevelt through the voices of children I hear you.

Ms. Keller through darkness and silence I hear you.

Ms. Mother Teresa through the sick, the poor, and the famished I hear you.

Ms. Parks

Ms. Thatcher

Ms. Truth

Ms. Tubman from the voices of freedom I hear you.

And I thank you for blossoming opportunities and comforting unspoken atrocities for young women and this world.

Now will you listen to their songs?

Or will you pull triggers executing the respect women are dying for?

"A" is for Art

Art is essential to life.

Begging for help won't release you from your plights.

Cat-call your conscience until your confidence lifts like a kite.

Dig a grave for fear and sing a prayer tonight.

Edify and elevate dead relatives still dying for your rights.

Forget fear and swallow faith like a shake.

Give your mistakes a chance to break.

Hold your dreams like a first born.

Ignite your passions like you meant to be born.

Jump from the bluff of faith and inhale tomorrow.

Kettle cook your forgiveness and X-hale your sorrows.

Let go of the past none have time to borrow.

Mimic the actions of God and be better.

Noose neck your pride and refuse the Devil's bribes.

Originality grows pure from the inside.

Purify your thoughts/ The God within you won't hide.

Quit compromising for the moment.

Risk everything for eternity.

Sacrifice the flesh for the spirit.

Teach everything to learn.

Understand before you speak.

Victory comes when you lose.

Weather the storm if it's Heaven you choose.

X-ray your heart/ God knows anyway.

Your dreams live within the palms of God.

Zap your temptations to silent and hear His whispers.

God Suffers

Some say

Sun rays

Peeking through these clouds

Is one of most beautiful sights

A pupil will possess.

It reminds me of hope

Held

Back against wall.

Only option is forward.

Pushing, scratching, striving

Still, stumbling like iron-leg words

Limping from my nervous lips.

We may trip, but faith found

Will never let us fall.

If struggle is progress, what clouds are we breaking?

That burning sun between your lungs beats over 100,000 times a day, what barriers are we breaking?

What cities are we shaking?

What lives are we saving by flat lining addictions?

What will you give when someone's soul needs lifting?

A promise for prayer?

Or

Contribute to Creation

Will you be, that landing between stairs of broken glass?

My grandmother's feet have more scars than the night has stars.

I don't need a telescope to tell the scope of her Trials.

She paved a path past racism

finished the trail

So I didn't have to do a mile.

She says, her grandchildren make her smile.

Her dawn after darkness

Her promise of Spring buried beneath Winter March's.

I don't need history 404 to help me remember Montgomery marches,

and aching arches bleeding stop

Only to hear the soul say forward

Echo through her thoughts like the birth of light rippling a horizon.

I'm thankful for that,

But it's not why I love her.

I love her because

When I was sick

She was there.

I love her because she loved me before I could say it back.

She believed in me before I could breathe on my own,

and she is not alone.

When my sister's heart was heavier than knees praying at their stillborn's tombstone.

She gave birth to perseverance

Because our past is rarely how we pictured when our present catches up to our future but that doesn't mean stop.

That means you just started.

So let's get started.

Never forgetting, forever remembering the names of the roots that irrigated your family tree.

My father says, "The Lord is always next to me."

Therefore,

There is No need chasing start lines

Manifested by worldly destinies.

He told me,

"God loves you more than me."

And that's hard to believe,

because he gave me more than

Just "needs."

Not worldly things.

Fleeting themes.

Or trinkets that gleam.

He gave me dreams.

He gave worth as a human being.

He gave me a future unseen,

and I didn't pay him anything

Contribute to Creation

Like a cathedrals lips puckering prayers

To the pillars of our hearts.

Stand straight

Bridge gaps,

and vertigo leap Dreams to a future full of promise

Like the thirsty lips of Jesus.

Nailed to a tree

33 years young.

Whimpering "it is done."

He didn't do it for fun.

Didn't do it for funds

He didn't do it for

Popularity or prosperity.

He did it because Love is long suffering

Like sentences saturated with hope

Pulling the wings of faith

Elevating forgotten-name angels

Baptized beneath the reach of God

God gave struggle to strengthen

Character.

Life isn't supposed to be easy.

When I was boy,

This is Why Kids Wanna Stay up Late

My Father made me cut grass

Below the Summer sun's heat.

I thought it was torture.

I use to tell my Dad, "I though slavery was over."

Now I know he was nurturing

The humility our hearts hunger for.

Like souls empty of empathy

Searching for Sundays to suck

Raisin dry.

Like Desert suns raised in the sky.

Despite the damaged days of our lives

Love survives.

God is the only picture of perfection we can look up to,

and His son died on a cross for heathens.

So when bad things happen to good people is there a need to ask for a reason.

Blessings are burdens

The burdens are blessings.

Slavery or secular success?

This poses yet,

Another question,

Which one will God Bless?

Aniyah

This is before your first breath.

My sister

Your mother

Our Father

Your Pops

Will love you,

Until they have nothing left,

To express affection they possess.

Even though you may not understand these words yet.

Accept this spoken token to the hope in

Your eyes dandelion dancing to whims of the wind.

Like

Dream-driven seeds

Staking roots

Family-tree.

You will always be a queen.

Whether or not you are on a movie screen

Voice casted for a summer Disney Fantasy.

Stand free

Anything you plan to be.

Just always have a plan B

Plan C

Plan D

Life gets tough

Like shrubs searching for sun below a canopy.

But when you fall

You have a family.

Support like

Stars holding planets and planets cradling moons.

When life throws typhoons,

We'll be there to tomb lock your worries away.

Now put on some Mickey Mouse,

It's time to play.

Hot Dog!

12:01

So, I'm dreaming of a lighthouse.

Cemented by innocent prayers.

Propelled from the lips of a gypsy kiss cursing concrete thoughts that think they know us best they don't.

Can we truly know bliss?

If we've never been broken

Broken like

Luckless limbs

On a rootless tree

Ravaged by ruthless winds.

Have you ever wanted your life to end? Is a question

That hangs

Thick heavy.

Like the news of your parents passing stone-stirred within the stew of sour syrup midnight darkness on a moonless night consumed by strife be moved by life.

Even if you feel like you could die twice

From the rape

From the touch

From the fist

From the words that ripped from your soul last night.

Reconsider.

This is a rebirth

This is a resurrection

When yesterday's horrors, trap your thoughts like a tomb.

This is the other side of gloom

Brighter than noon.

This is new beginnings beckoning to bloom

Like forgotten flowers frosted by February's breath.

This is the forgiveness machine.

This is the next step.

This is new friends you've met,

and their fingers filled with compassion

Reaching

Pushing you along when you have nothing left.

This is secrets you've kept,

but never could keep from God.

This is God's breath

Revitalizing the treble cleft

Next to your heart's sheet music.

This is a song for the broken

A song for the coping

A song for the hoping

A song for the many oceans

Of tomorrow's tears

Reflecting the past

Contribute to Creation

Like an emptied

Hourglass.

It is your time

Check the time

It is 12:01.

The other side of darkness, has already come.

Despite anxiety's tambourine tendencies

Shaking your bones like a California fault line

Sucking on syringes full of Red Bull.

Through your darkness I see light

Like your moon is full.

Through the halls of eyes, I see Heaven's glow

Dancing deliverance covered in the color of

Redemption.

There is no need to cover up the constellations captured within your irises.

This is where violence gives

Its final salute.

The hatred is moot.

And shame

Doesn't deserve access to your booth.

To vote or vie for your attention.

This is where ears always listen.

This is what we've all been missing.

This is Why Kids Wanna Stay up Late

You wanna see hope?

You are life after Chernobyl.

An ocean on Mercury.

Air in space.

You wanna see hope?

Go find a photo of your face.

Through your storm

Your life is a lighthouse.

A beacon begging the rest of us to hang on for just a little bit longer while our knuckles are bleeding,

because the darkness is receding

Like the moon was too heavy for the night to hold.

This is for the fires fueling your soul.

The burdens burning beneath your heart's charcoal

Will manifest manifolds of diamonds gleaming like

Tomorrow's promises.

This is no doubts.

It's easy to be faithless

If your life is unfamiliar with dark spaces.

This is for the forgotten faces, never found.

The uncrowned queens and kings

Ripped from their dreams

As if they had no worth.

This is a moment of silence for those who hurt.

A moment of silence

For the death of silence within our throats

When we hear a rape joke.

This is an insurrection against the media induced societal structural acceptance of violence against women the world promotes.

This is a new hope, without the lone Jedi.

This is living when the world said die

This is telling the truth within your testimony

When the world said lie.

Check the time.

It is 12:01.

The other side of darkness has already come.

Even if, your arduous journey to forgiveness and healing has just begun

Take the first step forward,

and you've already won.

This Moment

Throw your glasses up.

Like your pupils graduated from specs to contacts

Throw your glasses up.

Let's give a toast to love lost and love found,

and be thankful for another breath above ground.

If your pulse possesses a sound

Let me hear it from your throat

Like your heart had a concert.

The tickets were free,

Unlike the worse things in life.

Headline name

Juggling drums with an acrobat tongue.

If you are living, you are forever young.

This is for the songs of yesteryear

Our tears have sung for the ones we call loved ones.

When life is done and our breathe is gone,

What song will ring when lips of love sing?

What song will ring like the writhing rhythms of chains?

Shackled to souls

That grew hopeless instead of old.

What song will ring?

Contribute to Creation

When the lips of love sing like a mother's lullaby fingers light-dripping peace down your spine.

All your worries are benign, forever feeling fine

Let's find and dine within the depths of no regrets

No need to recollect steps

Step forward like God called your name.

The class is called the future

Pre-req is called the present

Discover meditation if you wish to learn your lesson.

We can't catch blessings if our hands are closed

Like the eyes of the moon when day lives or the hearts of southern racist.

Open your fingers like the ending of a prayer and prepare to receive like St. Nick is knocking on your wreath.

What song will ring like freedom frolicking from the lips of Dr. King when you open that letter of acceptance that possesses your favorite university's seal?

Name of the song,

"This Can't Be Real"

But it is.

What song will ring

When the lips of love sing

Like the sun clearing His throat

Expelling the dark specks on your soul?

What song will ring when the orphans of our eyes need someone to talk to?

This is Why Kids Wanna Stay up Late

What song will ring when the lips of love sing like silence

Between the lips of lovers

Connecting for the final time.

Only guarantee in life

Someone is always left behind.

So whether cancer took your

Mom or your Dad

My Aunt,

or that Uncle who could always make you laugh

Put a smile on your face like the veins of fein that just saw

His last day of rehab.

We have

The breath of tomorrow singing promise through the holes of our lungs like the wind-pipes of a 1926 Harlem Night.

Undeniable, irrevocable

We are here, in this moment!

Your tattered past reverberates

Ripples through every heartbeat to complete the perfect person you are now.

There is no better version certain, but that doesn't mean stop working.

The future is what you feed your soul

So,

Contribute to Creation

Throw your glasses up,

and let's give a toast to love lost and love found,

and be thankful for another breath above ground.

This stage called life is an opportunity to allow your voice to be heard.

Never fear it.

If your pulse possesses a sound, it is time to let the world hear it.